MW00638682

A
Quiet
Mind

Published in 2020 by OH!
An imprint of the Welbeck Publishing Group
20 Mortimer Street
London W1T 3JW

A CIP catalogue for this book is available from the British Library.

ISBN 978-1-78739-580-0

Printed in Italy

10 9 8 7 6 5 4 3 2 1

A Quiet Mind

BUDDHIST WAYS TO CALM THE NOISE IN YOUR HEAD

SHOUKEI MATSUMOTO

CONTENTS

INTRODUCTION

Are you troubled by the 'noise' that can be heard from all around in your day-to-day life?

Have you ever felt anger and jealousy well up at work, school or home, or felt like you just want to abandon all the negative things and escape somewhere?

This is a book for people who cannot find peace in their everyday lives. Let me start by introducing myself. I am Shoukei Matsumoto. In my search for the path to living well, I finally met Buddhist philosophy. After graduating from university, I dived into the world of temples and became a monk at Komyoji Temple, a Shin-Buddhist temple in downtown Tokyo. Now, as a travelling monk, I share Buddhist philosophy and practices with many people across the world.

With the exception of doing a slightly unusual job, I think my daily life isn't overly different from yours. I am neither an enlightened person nor a saint. I'm just your everyday layman and I hesitate to call myself a monk, strictly speaking.

But nevertheless, I have wandered far around the world of Buddhism, and it's thanks to this that I have become aware of rather a lot of things.

For example, I used to act in anger and greed, only doing things that hurt people and nature. But, as I have grown closer to Buddhism, I feel that I have gradually become more self-aware.

Rather than growing up, it was more a case of being stunned to see someone in the mirror who will never mature, and then using as much self-control as possible to minimize the damage done to others, taking care to stay calm and collected.

Although a little clumsily, I have so far been able to get by because of this. From deep within the heart of Buddhism comes a gentle guidance that is useful even to this layman.

In light of Buddhist teachings, this book contains my thoughts on how I myself, troubled by the 'noise' I hear from all around in my daily life, can keep a peaceful mind.

If the essence of Buddhism is useful in my everyday life, then surely anyone should be able to master it.

I would be delighted if this book were somehow able to help each of its readers move on to their next step.

Shoukei Matsumoto

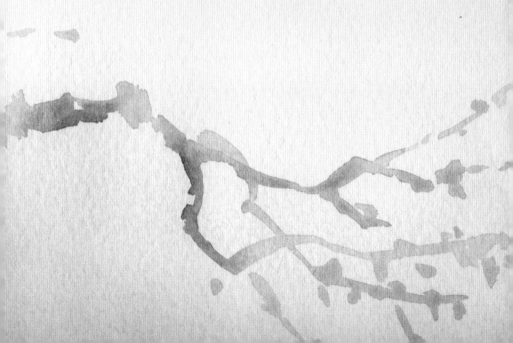

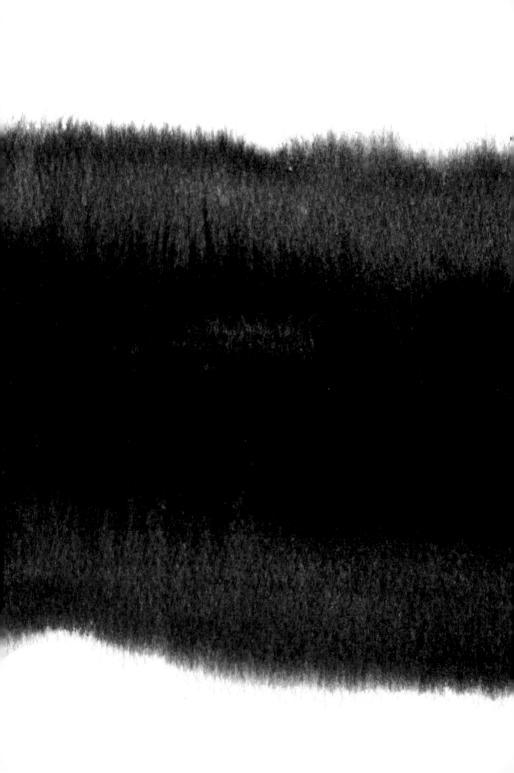

1
A NOISY
WORLD

DAYS FILLED
WITH NOISE

Nowadays, we are living in a truly noisy environment.

We rise out of bed to an alarm clock, listen to music through our headphones while we travel, and respond to the sounds of smartphones ringing from our pockets. Outside there are car horns and police sirens, and in many homes the television and radio are constantly switched on.

On top of all this, the environment we live in is considerably noisy to our eyes. Whether we look to the left or the right, information suddenly jumps out at us and catches our attention. When we go out to town there are new shops, when we take the train there are posters and banners, and when we get home there's the television and the internet. They all communicate new information to us without our asking, as and when they please.

THE WHIRLPOOL
OF DISTRACTION

Are we not living our lives surrounded by a considerable amount of noise? Let's look at this from a different angle. Imagine for a moment that you have one hour to focus on just one problem – for example, thinking about the theme of a report. Can you stay focused on the task without being disturbed by anything midway?

There are many sources of distraction even at home, such as telephone calls, emails and text messages and visits from delivery drivers. If you need to go into town to run a quick errand various things will entice you along the way and, as you stop off, an hour or so will pass by in what seems like a matter of seconds.

We have all had the same experience of getting nowhere with our work because we are doing something irrelevant, and then finding that our time is up. With the noise working against us, we are unable to think things through properly.

Of course, the noise in our society isn't something that began in this day and age.

Even hundreds of years ago, the towns were no doubt filled with distractions. Nevertheless, there has probably been no other time when the noise was as loud as it is now.

WE ALL NEED QUIET TIME

For better or worse, we happen to exist in an age where we lead very hectic lives.

With the development of various information and social media channels through the internet, the range of personal relationships and news that each person gets caught up in has dramatically expanded. There's so much new information and not enough time to organize it all, so we spend each day being busy.

Personally, I believe this is a rather dangerous situation. Through various experiences, human beings should be able to

It's a painful journey,
but a beautiful lotus
flower can bloom even
in the mud.

understand the world and steadily grow by calming the mind and considering things carefully. However, if we can't find any quiet time away from the noise, then we won't have the space to grow.

Even if we process a lot of information during our lives, no matter how long we live for, it will all come to nothing if we can't digest that information and learn from it.

We must look at ourselves and the things around us with a calm and peaceful mind, especially in this noisy age. It's important that we deepen our 'awareness' of the reality of the world and of ourselves.

LOOK OUTWARDS TO LOOK INWARDS

Constantly distracted by noise, when we try to look at ourselves we are somewhat unsuccessful. This is hardly surprising, since the human eye naturally faces outwards.

This is why we need a mirror, and Buddhism serves that purpose for me. It enables me to look out and look in at the same time.

It doesn't matter what you use as your mirror, so long as it fulfils that role properly. In my experience Buddhism works wonderfully well as it raises your awareness in smart and logical ways.

This awareness is essential to the development of the human mind, and Buddhism provides the natural yet highly effective nutrients that our growth depends upon.

One comment from a monk friend who practised severe asceticism stands out in my memory: 'Asceticism may be harsh, but it's not that harsh since what you ought to do is already decided.

The truly hard part comes after the ascetic practice ends and we return to this world.'

Indeed, that may be so. The training regime we must follow in this noise-filled environment is, in a sense, even more unforgiving than asceticism. It's a painful journey, but a beautiful lotus flower can bloom even in the mud.

Let Buddhism guide you through the difficulties of every day and along the path to peaceful awareness.

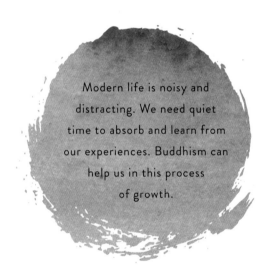

Modern life is noisy and distracting. We need quiet time to absorb and learn from our experiences. Buddhism can help us in this process of growth.

THE NOISES
FROM WITHIN

In our lives we are surrounded by a jumble of noise. But this noise doesn't just come from the outside – there's also the noise that comes from within which threatens our inner peace, such as that from jealousy and desire, anger and hatred. In fact, it is the noise from within that troubles our minds most violently.

Like commercials during movies, various external stimuli disturb our concentration without our realizing, but if we can somehow come to our senses we can regain that focus. However, this isn't so easy when the noise wells up from within.

For example, when we find out that someone has been saying bad things about us, what we hear comes from the outside and only passes through our ears for a moment. But when our minds react by saying, 'I can't forgive them for saying such things,' then the noise from within keeps ringing.

This isn't just when we react to insults. We often hold a selfish jealousy even towards those who are neither malicious nor guilty in any way. We may have thoughts such as 'I don't like how they stand out more than me' or 'I don't like how they're more fortunate than me.' Such noise is deeply rooted in the destructive emotions that lie within us, rather than coming from the outside.

RELEASE PENT-UP PRESSURE

When we don't like something or things don't go the way we want, the anger that comes with our suffering accumulates. We feel the stress building up in our minds like a gas, and when it reaches its limit there's a big explosion.

This is a terrible thing to happen, and so before it does I believe we must vent a little from time to time to release some of the tensions that have built up. In other words, try to reduce the noise that comes from within.

It's OK if we can refresh our minds by going on holiday or doing sports, but some people try to relieve their stress in ways that cause trouble for those around them.

For example, children who are stressed about studying for their exams might relieve that anxiety by bullying one of their classmates.

They might target those with good grades out of jealousy, or they might make fun of those who have lower grades than themselves. The false impression that they are the only ones suffering makes them want to inflict suffering on others.

There are similar situations even in the world of adults. Although we may think someone is a good person, behind closed doors they might be violent or use abusive language towards certain colleagues and subordinates, or they might victimize others by leaving them out of the group.

But if we think calmly it becomes clear that acting in this way will do anything but reduce the noise within our minds – rather, it will increase it further and threaten our inner peace.

If you want to eliminate the noise from within, you have to look closely at the cause.

We feel the stress building up in our minds like a gas, and when it reaches its limit there's a big explosion.

THE 'THREE POISONS':
RAGA, DVESHA AND MOHA

In Buddhist teachings, the destructive emotions *raga*, *dvesha* and *moha*, collectively known as the 'three poisons', are said to be the cause of our suffering.

- *Raga* is a mind of greed and an attachment to material items.
- *Dvesha* is a mind of anger that becomes enraged.
- *Moha* is a mind of delusion and loss of self through instinct and desire.

It is said that by controlling these three emotions, we will overcome the evils and suffering of humanity.

From a Buddhist point of view, stress builds up when we are swayed by *raga*, *dvesha* and *moha*. We then become angry when things don't go the way we expect, and when that anger reaches boiling point we lose sight of ourselves and instinctively lash out at others, aggravating the situation even more.

Rather than resolving the problem, acting on the anger that fills our hearts by using violence towards others amplifies the effect of the three poisons, and we do nothing but fall into the depths of confusion.

It's impossible for bullying and other such actions to clear and refresh our minds. The more we take these actions, the more our minds stagnate and the heavier the negative feelings become. Although we seem to be aware of this, these destructive emotions are strong enough to mislead us. Outside stimuli can also awaken the noise of jealousy and anger from within. If we are unaware of the circumstances in which such negative emotions arise, then we may find that we are unable to deal with them, further amplifying the noise and increasing our worries.

If you want to lead a peaceful life, try to pay careful attention not just to noise from the outside but also to the noise that wells up from within.

Internal noise from negative emotions can be more harmful than external noise. Find a healthy way to release stress before it explodes. Taking your stress out on others just makes things worse for everyone. Try to understand the external causes of negative emotions.

ACHIEVING
STILLNESS

Although I say obtain a 'quiet mind', it's not always necessary for us to head to a world where there are no physical sounds.

For those of us who don't live in a secluded mountain retreat, the quiet mind we need will be useless unless we are able to find it within the hubbub of everyday life.

Some people may think that it's impossible to have a quiet mind in a busy city. But, the amazing thing about human beings is that we can change our own consciousness.

When we take in noise from the outside that we find unpleasant we can go one step further by noticing the very change within our minds. And so even while living in a busy city we should be able to find peace in the middle of the hustle and bustle by exercising our consciousness a little.

As an example, different people may hear the same words from the same person at the same time and interpret those words completely differently. Some will take them as a compliment, while others will take them as a snide remark. Or where people get the same wages, some will think it's a lot of money, while others will think it's not.

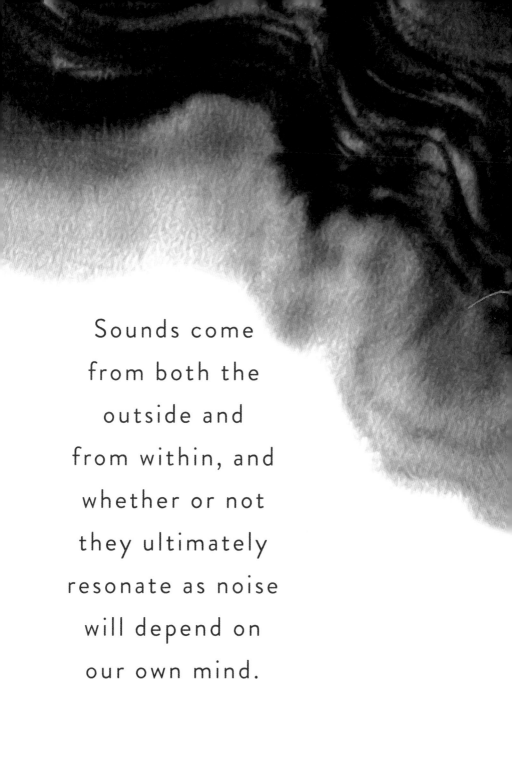

Sounds come
from both the
outside and
from within, and
whether or not
they ultimately
resonate as noise
will depend on
our own mind.

CHANGE YOUR INTERPRETATION
NOT YOUR LOCATION

Our surroundings depend on our way of thinking. Of course, it can be good to actually change our surroundings by going away, but that's not a lasting solution to the problem.

Even if we think for a moment that we've found the ideal location without any noise, after a while things will revert to the way they were before. This is because nothing has changed within us. If we don't change the way we interpret sounds, then the world we look upon will remain clouded no matter where we go.

Thinking of a place where there's no noise, we might believe that if we head to the mountains, for example, then we won't hear any voices or car sounds, right? Indeed, that may be true. If we head out hiking in the mountains on our days off, we can enjoy a natural environment without any artificial noise.

However, such places are not for everyday living. Above all, if we have serious problems within our lives we cannot escape from them by heading to the mountains or the sea.

Sounds come from both the outside and from within, and whether or not they ultimately resonate as noise will depend on our own mind.

How we react to the sounds we hear is a major issue. By having all sorts of experiences, we develop patterns of response towards various stimuli.

It's the same as Pavlov's dogs. In that famous behavioural experiment, a bell was rung whenever it was time for food, and eventually the dogs would drool just at the sound of the bell. The older we get, the more patterns we accumulate, and so in one sense our way of life becomes more stable.

However, in the opposite sense it means that the number of opportunities we have to feel the freshness of experiencing things for the first time steadily reduces. This may be the reason why many people say that as they get older time seems to quicken as if passing by in a geometric progression.

DO NOT LET SOUND BECOME NOISE

'There's so much noise all around me and there's no way out!' It's possible that people who feel like this have developed a circuit within their mind that causes any sounds they hear to be felt as 'noise'.

Buddhism is said to teach mindfulness, and one characteristic of Buddhism is that it grants an awareness to those who come into contact with its teachings.

I have spent years in a Buddhist environment, and within a period of time the part which resonates with me has changed depending on the moment. This has granted me a lot of new awareness, changing the way I feel towards things.

This book invites you to contemplate how to live your daily life quietly and peacefully, and this 'awareness' is essential for that.

First of all, it's an awareness that there's no place free from sound. We cannot escape from sound itself.

It's also an awareness that whether or not we hear these sounds as 'noise' depends entirely upon ourselves. In other words, if we can change the way we listen then what we thought of as noise will be detoxified into clear sounds.

To have a quiet mind you do not need quiet surroundings, you just need to change your interpretation of the sounds in your environment. Accept that these sounds are inevitable and they will cease to be a noisy distraction.

A NOISY WORLD

SEEING THINGS AS THEY TRULY ARE

Both outside and within, there's no place that's free from sound. We talked about how the problem lies within ourselves, as we are the ones who hear the 'noise'. So why is it that we are unable to hear sound simply as sound? It's because we can't see things as they truly are.

There are people who can't quite see despite their efforts, and there are others who simply look away without trying. There are also many who are convinced they can see, even though they can't.

For example, when I look at a river flowing before me I think, 'There's a river here.' However, what's actually there is water and, what's more, it's constantly changing so it's never the same water that flows even for a moment. Looking at the dynamic movement of the water, I foolishly believe that the river never changes.

Again, when I look at the two books on the desk in my study I think, 'This book is mine; that one I borrowed.'

Indeed, there is no mistaking that I bought the one and borrowed the other. However, what's actually there is two books that just happen to be on top of the desk, and this has absolutely nothing to do with who either the desk or the books belong to.

But when I look at the two books, I am intently aware of their ownership and differentiate between them accordingly.

It seems to be the same with regards to our own bodies. While we are alive the cells of our bodies continue to be replaced many times over. The changes are so small that they're difficult to notice from one day to the next, but our bodies visibly change over time.

We get more wrinkles, our hair falls out and we become physically weaker. But people desperately try to resist these changes and put their best efforts into slowing down the ageing process.

First and foremost, humans don't even attempt to look at their own lives face on. When attending the funeral of a dear friend we think, 'They were still so young, it's such a shame.' And we don't really consider how a similar fate also awaits us one day. While we are aware that the mortality rate of humans is one hundred per cent, it's normal for us to completely overlook this fact. Even if we do remember every once in a while, we pretend to forget and avert our eyes from the truth.

Buddhism
teaches us
'acceptance',
which doesn't
mean to abandon
hope but rather
to see things
clearly.

LOOK BEYOND DESTRUCTIVE EMOTIONS

Although humans are the most intelligent living creatures on earth, our intelligence affords us no more than a small amount of wisdom and we are unable to see things as they truly are.

So how can we gain the ability to see the 'truth'? We'll have to jump over many hurdles to find our way to it, right?

Actually, that's not so. The truth is the truth, and it lies before our eyes whenever or wherever we are. It has been said many times, but the problem resides within us as we can only interpret things through our own selfishness.

It is our selfishness that causes us to hear sounds not simply as sounds but rather as 'noise'.

In Buddhism, what prevents us from recognizing things as they truly are is our destructive emotions. For example, despite living in a world where nothing remains the same and everything is constantly changing, people don't actually want things to change.

LEARN TO ACCEPT

It's unlikely that life will go the way you expect, and trying to have your own way can become painful.

So how can you solve the problem of life not turning out the way you want? The answer that Buddhism teaches us is 'acceptance', which doesn't mean to abandon hope but rather to see things clearly.

What's important is to clearly assess the state of your life, which will never be exactly the way we want it.

But this isn't easy to do. While we may try to be mindful of the fact that things will never go the way we want, even this doesn't go as we expect. However, there is a considerable difference in our mental capacity for handling the worry that things don't go the way we want, and the worry of actually knowing that something won't go the way we want.

If our minds aren't calm and peaceful, then the noise from our own selfishness will increase more and more, constantly moving us further from the truth.

There are truths that our selfishness stops us from seeing clearly. One is that everything is constantly changing, including ourselves. Another is that things will never turn out the way we want. Accepting these truths will help to quieten our minds.

STAYING
CALM

We find it very difficult to see things as they truly are. Our destructive emotions get in the way and all we hear is noise. Like the Buddha, if we could completely eliminate those destructive emotions we would no longer be troubled by unpleasant sounds – but this is hard for us to do.

However, it's due to our selfishness that sounds which were originally neutral are heard as noise. Even just recognizing that truth will start to calm our minds and can set in motion various changes within our lives.

BREAK OUT OF THE VICIOUS CIRCLE

With a calmer mind, one change we will notice is that we start to make fewer mistakes at work or in our studies. At times when concentration is essential it's frustrating when we are unable to

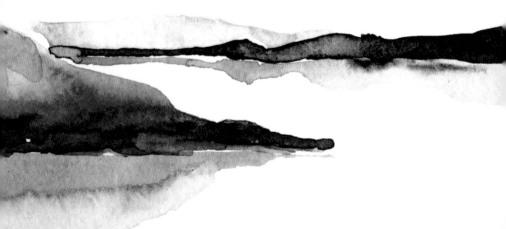

focus properly, and this in turn means we steadily become less and less able to do so, trapped in a vicious circle. In situations like this if you can try to stay calm, search for the cause of your frustration and gather your emotions it will lead to a positive outcome.

Professional baseball pitchers often say that the positive results they get when they're in good form mean less to them than the times they have managed to hold things together when they have not been feeling so good. If you have an objective awareness of your own current state and are able to deal with it calmly, then everything will naturally have a positive flow.

In contrast, act with caution when your mind is troubled or you feel emotional, and you're unable to make calm decisions and see your surroundings clearly.

You may meet people who unsettle the weakened parts of your mind and successfully deceive you. You may also lose sight of yourself and cause trouble by misdirecting your anger towards others.

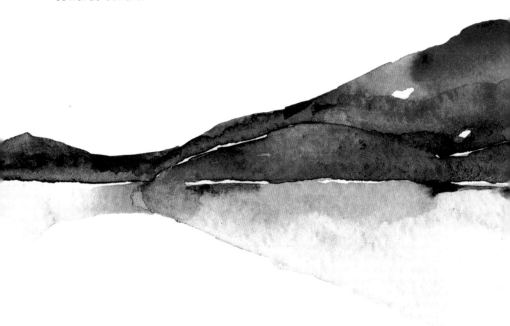

This can lead to the people who are important to you drifting away, leaving bad company to fill the void. When this happens, the noise increases, the quiet life is lost and you become trapped within a vicious circle where noise calls for more noise.

STEP BACK FROM YOUR ANGER

When exactly does the volume of noise grow? I believe this is when we are filled with anger.

Anyone can fly into a rage when triggered by a disagreement. I have also had times like this where I have lost my senses and, in spite of myself, have used abusive language that I come to regret. This regret usually comes afterwards, as it's not something we readily feel in the moment when our minds are being controlled by our emotions. It's only after we have collected ourselves and begun to recover our senses that we can acknowledge our faults and feel remorse.

When you think that you are about to be controlled by your emotions like this, first take a deep breath, calm your feelings and focus on recovering your senses. Look at yourself through the eyes of an outsider. 'No matter how you look at it, you're not to blame.' If you tell yourself this, then you'll think carefully first and protest later, calming yourself down for the time being.

Once you have calmed down search for a way to solve the problem. But don't be mistaken – the solution isn't to prove that the other person is wrong and you are right. Rather, it's important that we each consider things from the other person's perspective.

That being said, this doesn't mean you should do whatever the other person tells you to do. Naturally, you must try and think calmly, and if there's still something that doesn't sit right, point out exactly what it is and object in an appropriate manner.

However, when the other person is overcome with rage and anger, nothing good will come to either party if your only thought is to get the better of them. Only when there is stillness of the mind can human relationships become fruitful.

Now then, the teachings of Buddhism are difficult and you may believe that they're not particularly useful for real-life situations, such as arguments with other people. But that isn't the case. Actually, Buddhism contains a treasure trove of hints about human life that are immediately useful within our own lives.

Let's now take a look at how to obtain a quiet mind by exploring these clues found in Buddhism.

The first step to calmness is recognizing destructive emotions within us. Then we can take a step back to understand the cause of our anger or frustration and neutralize it before it traps us in a vicious circle.

2
QUIET
TIME

FINDING
QUIET TIME

Do you live with other people, or do you live on your own?

Those who live alone have plenty of time to themselves, but I think that even those who value spending time with their families or housemates also like to have some personal space.

Spending our time how we want to without any interruptions is relaxing, and if we don't find time like this every once in a while we won't be able to think carefully about any of the things that are important to us.

TURN OFF THE TV

Finding quiet time alone can require a certain discipline. Even if we live by ourselves, we may not give ourselves the opportunity to spend time alone in its true sense.

For example, I believe there are quite a lot of people who turn on the television as soon as they get home.

If you switch it on and leave it on, then entertainers, presenters, politicians and celebrities will appear one after another, laughing at scripted stories, discussing social issues and announcing the news.

For those who live alone, the television can be a convenient and comforting tool to distract them from their loneliness. However, it can also prevent us from having any time at home to ourselves.

If you make a point of only watching programmes you are actively interested in you can still have some time to yourself. But, if you make a habit of turning on the television as soon as you get in without any particular reason and then only turn it off when you go to bed, the people on your screen aren't just the ones you talk and have fun with but also the ones who put you to sleep at night. This is by no means quiet time to yourself.

Newspapers and magazines are another form of media, but, unlike television, they don't address us directly on their own. They can't be read simply by us noticing them; we need to make the effort to read them ourselves. With the TV, everything is done for us – including getting our attention.

The way we passively and unconsciously receive information poses the risk of awakening our desires without our even noticing. Moreover, when somebody else's agenda is strong at work within that information it is of no benefit to us – and may even have a negative impact on the peace of our day-to-day lives.

At the very least, we want to try turning off the TV when it has been switched on for no particular reason.

USE YOUR QUIET TIME WELL

Now, if you have been able to get your distractions under control and find some quiet time, please go ahead and spend it as you wish.

That being said, it would be a waste to laze around and idle away this precious time. There's no question that we want to be using this time to concentrate on something.

If you're someone who wants to master a foreign language, then you should use this time for studying. If you have documents that you need to write, then use it for work. It's also good to use this time for yoga, tai chi or anything that gets your body moving.

As for monks, there are those who might read sutras and think about Buddhism. In short, as long as you concentrate on what you think you should – and must – be doing at that moment, then whatever you do is fine.

If you concentrate on something even for just a short amount of time your mind will be refreshed and you'll feel more focused. Plus, if you use that short amount of time to concentrate on what you need to get done at that moment, you will gain peace of mind.

When I rise early to read sutras and focus on my thoughts I often find that for the rest of the day I am able to keep any feelings of tension at a reasonable level and my day goes well.

Keep making as much effort as you can. Rather than casually turn on the TV, why not get into the habit of having some quiet time to yourself and focusing on something?

We all need quiet
time alone to collect our
thoughts, but being physically
alone doesn't guarantee us quiet
time. Turn off the TV if it is on for no
reason and use the time instead to
focus on an absorbing mental
or physical activity.

CONSCIOUS
BREATHING

We have probably all had at least one experience in our lives where we have got worked up and been unable to sleep the night before doing something like giving an important presentation, or where our hands and feet have gone rigid and we've been unable to get our words out properly while standing before an audience. When your mind is agitated, so is your body.

I have never been particularly good at speaking in front of people. Since I have had more opportunities to do Buddhist sermons I have become a little more used to it, but I still get nervous.

When we get nervous, our blood pressure rises, we sweat, and our breathing becomes shallow and fast. A mental change also has a physical impact. It feels like we have no control over our bodies, leaving us all the more troubled when we have something important to do. However, there are a number of actions that we can control, even among those that our bodies are unconsciously doing every day. One of them is breathing.

TAKE A DEEP BREATH

Our bodies usually breathe automatically without our consciously thinking, 'Breathe in, breathe out.' But if you're aware of your breathing, you can take slow, deep breaths.

Take notice of this and you'll understand why people say to first take a deep breath when you're feeling nervous. By taking a deep breath your body can relax and you can get yourself back into shape, thereby relieving mental tension and regaining a sense of peace.

In the West the mind and body are traditionally regarded as separate, but in the East they are seen as one inseparable, balanced whole. At the heart of this is breathing.

Buddhism has a form of thinking known as the 'middle way', a balanced frame of mind that avoids extremes (see page 151). The Buddha went through a period of rigorous asceticism that pushed his body to the very limit, until eventually even he abandoned austerity and found enlightenment instead through quiet meditation.

When his body was filled with pain he was unable to achieve the state of mind that he attained by calming his body, controlling his breathing, and meditating.

CONTROL YOUR BODY
TO CONTROL YOUR MIND

It is said that a monk who has properly trained and disciplined his mind and body for many years will be able to control both quite freely.

They are skilled at keeping their mind calm by suppressing feelings such as irritation or jealousy, and they become able to take long, deep breaths without having to think about it. It seems there are even those who reach the point where they are consciously able to change body functions that normal people are unable to control, such as perspiration and heart rate.

If you can master these you'll be able to freely manipulate how the mind interacts with the body and the body with the mind.

Come to think of it, there are many who live a long life among the masters of Buddhism. The Buddha himself lived until he was eighty years old, while Shinran, the founder of Shin Buddhism, lived until he was ninety. These were both extraordinarily long lives for their times – roughly twice the average life expectancy.

This was likely down to habits such as eating in moderation and walking long distances on missionary work, but a full heart and calm disposition would also have been important factors.

Human beings are composed of a mind and body constantly working together. In order to live a healthy and peaceful life we must be mindful of the movements in both.

The key to uniting mind and body is our breath.

For a long time now Japanese people have had a sense of just how important the breath is to humans. In the Japanese language, the character for breath is 息 (iki), and there are countless expressions that use this character. These include 息が合う (*iki ga au*), which means 'to get along smoothly', and 息を抜く (*iki wo nuku*), meaning 'to take a break'. For the Japanese, breath is life itself. Being conscious of our breath – something we usually take for granted – leads to a renewed awareness of its importance.

It also seems that Japan's past prime ministers were able to control their breathing and calm their minds through *zazen*, a type of seated meditation practice. Nowadays, many Japanese businessmen can be seen in the meditation halls of Zen Buddhist temples. If you can open your eyes to your mind and body through your breath you may come upon peace.

The mind and body are a single entity. Changes in one affect the other, so, for example, when your mind is agitated your body responds with increased heart rate and perspiration and faster, shallower breathing. Conscious, deep breathing is the key to restoring calm to your body – and your mind.

ESCAPING THE
HUSTLE AND BUSTLE

Where is your quiet place you can relax? I feel at ease when I escape from the hustle and bustle of the city and take a walk in nature. I especially like places where there's water.

When I hear the sound of waves lapping against the shore I think about the insignificance of my everyday problems and my heart is liberated. Nature's rhythms awaken my spirit and give me a sense of peace. But the calming sounds of oceans and rivers are unexpectedly loud. Water in nature can create such a thunderous roar that we are unable to hear others speak. Despite this, for some reason I feel completely at peace near water.

In other words, not all places that help to quieten our minds are themselves quiet. What allows us to calm our minds in a particular spot is that all the various elements there are in harmony.

FIND PEACE IN A TEMPLE

I think temples are ideal locations for composing the mind, since they were originally created as places for monks to train.

In order for monks to devote themselves to their training, the environment must be suitable for focusing the mind. For this reason, temples generally have a calming atmosphere; I have never heard of one that causes the minds of visitors to grow restless.

Many of the visitors to Kyoto's famous temples are not there as tourists but as people searching for a place that can help heal their minds. We often catch sight of them staying at the temple for a while without doing anything in particular, simply sitting on the veranda or strolling in the grounds, taking in the atmosphere.

For those people, temples are not places for sightseeing – they are places to spend time.

I myself am one of those people who enjoy temples in this way. When I find one that I like, I wonder, 'Why is this place so peaceful? What does it have that my home doesn't?'

I then search for elements that I think I could incorporate into my own home and try to take these ideas back with me.

This may seem impossible since the ambiance of a temple is completely different from that of a home, but it is less different than you might think. A temple's calming nature does not come from a secluded setting or ancient architecture, neither of which is available to those of us who live in modern, urban dwellings. Instead, a large part of a temple's atmosphere comes from the great care taken by those who look after it, and from the warmth of the Buddha – and these are qualities that you can bring into your home.

MAKE YOUR HOME LIKE A TEMPLE

A pleasant temple is one that has been cleaned thoroughly from corner to corner, and where you can sense a careful consideration towards visitors. There are also no unnecessary objects to be found and all the necessary items are placed exactly where they're

What allows us to calm our
minds in a particular spot is
that all the various elements
there are in harmony.

needed, nothing is inconvenient. All of this is done by those who maintain the temple. There's nothing mysterious here; you can do all these things at home if you put your mind to it.

It's also possible that some people think temples are special because they are where Buddha resides, but you can welcome Buddha into your home by installing a Buddhist altar. Known as a *butsudan*, this is a place where Buddha is traditionally enshrined. In fact, a Buddhist altar is a miniature temple within the home.

Please cherish the places where you feel a deep sense of harmony. They are not just places to relax, but also places where you feel so free that you're able to be your true self. They are an irreplaceable treasure.

Seek out the places that bring you peace. This might involve walking in nature or visiting a temple. You can re-create the atmosphere of a temple in your home by keeping it clean, tidy and well-ordered, showing consideration towards your visitors and installing a Buddhist altar.

WALKING

When we experience a great setback we often lose our self-confidence. We may think that we won't be able to get back on our own two feet, or we may feel like nobody needs us. Obsessed with negative thoughts we become unable to move forward.

But even during times like these there is a way for us to keep moving forward with certainty, and that is by walking. If we can use our own strength to place our feet on the ground and make steady progress with each step, then little by little we will regain our momentum.

GO ON A
PILGRIMAGE

Walking is an ideal way to calm our minds and reflect on ourselves. Many people, not only monks, take pilgrimages like the Shikoku in southern Japan. These very long walks have become popular journeys of self-discovery.

The small exchanges we have with the people we meet along the way also play a role in restoring our hope for humanity. Like this, we can calm the mind and move forward.

Of course, it goes without saying that walking is also good for your physical health.

Advocating the merits of solitary asceticism to reach enlightenment, the Buddha himself once said, 'Wander alone, like the rhinoceros,' and after reaching enlightenment at the age of thirty-five he walked all over India preaching to the people. He continued do this in earnest until his death forty-five years later

It must have been a very long and severe path, and it's possible he was only able to accomplish such a journey until the age of eighty because he continued walking on his own two feet. By following the Buddha's example of continuing to do a reasonable amount of regular exercise at a steady pace, we, too, can maintain a balance between the body and the mind throughout our lives.

THE *SENNICHI KAIHOGYO*: A SERIOUS WALK

There are numerous walking practices in Buddhism, the most extreme of which is a thousand-day walk around Kyoto's Mount Hiei known as the *Sennichi Kaihogyo*. This is famous as one of the most severe walking practices in the world.

The thousand days of walking are spread over seven years. During each of the first three years, practitioners spend 100 days walking around Mount Hiei for 40 kilometres a day. And there isn't just walking involved – they must also visit 255 pilgrimage sites every day, which means that for the most part they try to run.

For the duration of the practice the meals are very plain and simple, which is what the body needs to be able to keep walking day after day.

In the fourth and fifth years the number of walking days doubles to 200 per year. After the fifth year, by which time they will have completed 700 days, the monk must carry out a ritual known as *doiri*, which means 'entering the hall'. They go without food, water or rest of any kind for the next nine days, in order to become one with the protective deity Acala.

In the sixth year the number of walking days reverts to 100, but the daily distance increases to 60 kilometres and the route extends beyond Mount Hiei. In the seventh year, they walk 84 kilometres a day for 100 days, taking a pilgrimage route around the temples and shrines within the city of Kyoto, before walking 30 kilometres a day in the mountains for the final 100 days.

The total distance covered over those thousand days of walking is actually 40,000 kilometres – roughly the same distance as going once around the Earth. What's more, Yusai Sakai, a monk who lived a long and healthy life until his death in 2013 at the age of eighty-seven, successfully completed this practice twice. He is only the third person to have achieved this remarkable feat.

The difficulty of this training is beyond imagination – in fact, monks attempting the *Sennichi Kaihogyo* face the challenge prepared to die. They wear white clothing, the colour worn to Buddhist funerals, and attach both a rope and a dagger to their waist to be used to take their own life if they are unable to complete the practice.

Of course, when the act of walking is taken this far it no longer becomes a question of maintaining physical and mental health. But it goes to show the significance that is ascribed to walking as a spiritual practice.

If we can use our own strength to place our feet on the ground and make steady progress with each step, then little by little we will regain our momentum.

FEEL THE GROUND UNDER YOUR FEET

I love walking and if I have time I'll head out for a stroll. Whether in the city or the countryside, I walk at a steady pace and try to find roads I don't know. But there are fewer things to distract your attention on country routes, so I find them better for calming my mind and organizing my thoughts.

In the city, crowds and traffic lights hinder your progress. The walking surface is nothing but tarmac and concrete, which makes the feeling of your feet hitting the ground a little artificial. In the countryside you can walk on fields and dirt roads, which I prefer.

Try going for a steady walk, either along country paths or through a large city park with plenty of soil underfoot. There are unexpected discoveries to be made in nature.

Steady, regular walking is an ideal way to calm your mind and organize your thoughts. A long walk, or even pilgrimage, can restore your momentum and help you regain your confidence step by step after a setback.

WRITING

I have been writing blog posts since I became a monk about six years ago now, and in other forms for much longer than that.

Writing doesn't just help you record your thoughts and tell people what you think. By documenting the thoughts that float into your mind and then organizing them logically you can discover new perspectives.

SHOW YOUR WORKINGS

When your head is clouded, my advice is simply to try writing something – not for other people to read but for you to deepen your own understanding.

Long ago, only a select number of intellectuals could read and write. These included the monks who traditionally read and wrote the sutras. For example, Shinran spent a lot of his life writing and left behind many pieces of work.

What is particularly remarkable is that, centuries later, we can trace his thought process through his writing. There are sections where we can see that he has added to or amended his sentences. It seems that Shinran wrote his thoughts as they came to him, read over what he had written, thought once more, and then made revisions.

I dare say he found this process extremely useful not just as a way to convey his thoughts to others as clearly as possible but also to help him deepen those thoughts for his own benefit.

Shinran didn't just write about the philosophical complexities of Buddhism. Using poetic language, he also directly expressed his own joy in finding Buddhism. We can enjoy his writing purely as literature, appreciating not just the development of his thoughts but also of his emotions.

Throughout our daily lives, we are more pleased and saddened by matters relating to our relationships and the results of our work and study, rather than by Buddhism. Writing about these matters is a good way to understand changes in our emotions. For this reason, writing your feelings down is also a method used in psychotherapy.

WRITE YOUR WRONGS

In Buddhism, human actions can be classified as those of the body (physical), the mouth (verbal) and the mind (mental). In each of these categories we are capable of acting sinfully.

Sins of the body include killing other living creatures and stealing. Those of the mouth include lies, slander and flattery. Those of the mind include thinking impure thoughts and losing our temper.

Trying not to do these sinful acts will result in a peaceful mind. But this is easier said than done, and here again writing can help us – particularly when it comes to dealing with sins of the mind.

Everybody is going to think about doing bad things, but it is possible to avoid committing misdeeds of the body and the mouth. You may be driven by a desire to do them, but more often than not you can somehow suppress the urge before thought becomes action.

However, it's difficult to deny misdeeds of the mind. We cannot erase sinful thoughts from within our heads. So how should we go about controlling something that has already entered our consciousness?

One way is to completely ignore what enters our minds. Even if we have angry thoughts, leave them as they are and think no more about them. Then, at the very least, they will not physically or verbally manifest themselves in the form of violence or insults.

Another way is to accept whatever enters our minds and properly digest it. Don't ignore feelings of anger, for example, but instead face up to those emotions by acknowledging that you're currently angry and then searching for the cause.

Personally, I think the latter approach offers a way to deepen our understanding and move forward, particularly if we examine our negative feelings by writing them down.

Ignoring our own emotions doesn't allow us to deepen our understanding, and it isn't a fundamental solution. The same thing is likely to happen all over again in the future. However, although it takes a lot of time and effort, by confronting our thoughts and finding a more constructive way of thinking, those misdeeds of the mind should gradually become fewer and fewer.

In order to live a peaceful life, you must first know your own mind. In that respect, writing your feelings down on paper is an effective way to be true to yourself.

If any negative emotions rise up from within you try writing them down. As you search for the cause and face your true feelings your mind should naturally become calm.

Writing is not only a means of communication with others but also a way to gain a deeper understanding of our thoughts and feelings. Confront your negative thoughts: write them down and then write down an alternative, more constructive way of thinking

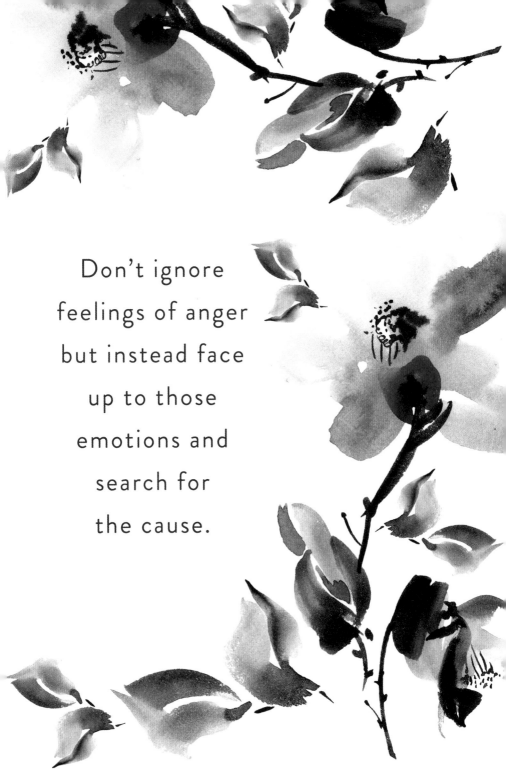

Don't ignore
feelings of anger
but instead face
up to those
emotions and
search for
the cause.

SUTRAS

For many Japanese people, sutras are the first thing that comes to mind when we think of Buddhism.

Today, funerals and memorial services are the main occasions when ordinary people engage with Buddhism and these may be the only occasions where they hear sutras being recited. Therefore, many people associate sutras with sad situations. But actually, at their core, sutras aren't something to be saddened by. They are concentrated capsules of wisdom to be read and enjoyed, bringing more happiness than sorrow.

Needless to say, they can be read anywhere, even outside of temples. In the past, there were many families who would gather daily in front of their Buddhist altars to read sutras.

I remember that my grandfather could barely recall any recent events, but amazingly he could still remember the sutras he read with his family in front of the altar when he was a child.

However, those who have never read a sutra probably won't know where to begin. If that's the case, why not start by going to a temple?

In recent years, there has been a boom in practices that familiarize us with sutras, such as *shomyo*, a type of Buddhist chant, and *shakyo*, the copying out of the sutras. Why not try introducing yourself to the sutras little by little?

GENTLE TEACHINGS AND
TALES OF GRATITUDE

What is actually written in the sutras?

There may be some people who are scared of them since they contain lines and lines of difficult kanji, looking almost like a magic spell. This supernatural aura is compounded by the many legendary tales of monsters being vanquished when struck by paper talismans on which sutras have been written.

However, in reality, it's not spells that are written in the sutras. Instead sutras contain the gentle teachings of the Buddha, as well as Buddhist tales of gratitude compiled by his disciples.

From the time when he reached enlightenment at the age of thirty-five right up to his death at the age of eighty, the Buddha travelled around India preaching. Moreover, the Buddha told his truths in a way that was accessible to all those he was preaching to. Therefore, the content of the sutras varies greatly, from philosophical writings to stories.

There are so many sutras that later generations found it hard to choose which ones to read. To solve this problem, great monks of the past came forward and made selections from the vast number available. For example, the Three Pure Land Sutras were selected by Honen Shonin, founder of Jodo Buddhism, and these sutras are cherished by both the Jodo Buddhist and Shin Buddhist sects of Pure Land Buddhism.

Sutras contain the gentle
teachings of the Buddha,
as well as Buddhist tales
of gratitude compiled
by his disciples.

ENJOY THE RHYTHM OF SUTRAS

While we are on the subject, when I was a child and there were memorial services and such taking place at the temple I would think to myself, 'What's the point in reading out something you don't understand, and that's filled with nothing but kanji?'

But I don't think this as much anymore. Of course, it's best to read the sutras while also studying the content but it isn't just their meaning that is important – I have come to realize that the sounds and rhythm themselves also have the power to awaken our emotions.

For example, I once went and listened to a *shomyo* chant of the Tendai sect at a public performance. It had a distinctive tune and I was amazed by its rich melody. The performance as a whole had a narrative, and I felt that it was also a powerful piece of theatre. I suppose we could also say it's a traditional art that has been nurtured in Mount Hiei.

In the Otani sect of Shin Buddhism there is a tradition known as *bando-bushi*, which is still practised today. It is said to date from the time when Shinran was exiled to Echigo Province, now Niigata Prefecture. While being rocked by the raging waves he chanted the name of Amitabha, the great saviour Buddha.

Dozens of monks perform *bando-bushi* in unison. Sitting on tatami mats, they violently shake only their upper bodies while loudly chanting the name of Amitabha. It's an extremely powerful performance, and you can't help but be overwhelmed by it.

A POWERFUL EXPRESSION OF UNITY

The most moving sutras of all are those that you yourself read aloud with a group of friends in a temple.

Sutras are the words of the Buddha and if you read them in unison with other people you will feel as though you're all disciples listening to his teachings as a single body. This brings a strong sense of unity and the whole temple is filled with a deep, indescribable emotion.

Often recited in Buddhist ceremonies such as funerals, sutras are the collected teachings of the Buddha. They may also be read alone or among family and friends. Through both their meaning and their rhythm they can have a profound effect on the mind and emotions.

EARLY MORNING
ROUTINES

If you were told to participate in temple training for a week, what would be the hardest part?

Kneeling in the *seiza* position with your feet tucked under looks painful, the meals look like they wouldn't be enough and the rules seem strict. I think there are all sorts of difficulties, but the one thing that people probably regard as particularly challenging is the early morning lifestyle, having to rise before the break of day.

I used to be one of those people. However, when I tried implementing an early morning routine I felt well both physically and mentally. If I'd known I would spend my days feeling so refreshed I would have started getting up earlier long before I did and I regret that I didn't.

Having some quiet time to yourself in the early morning leaves you with a sense of peace throughout the rest of the day.

It all began when Kenjitsu Nakagaki, a priest living in New York, taught me that getting up early would feel good and that I would also make progress in my work, so if I were able to pick up the pace life would become very comfortable.

No matter what, it's important that we keep up the pace.

GET A HEAD START ON YOUR DAY

My routine consists of going to bed around eleven or twelve o'clock at night, and then waking up at half past five in the morning.

It might seem like the time we gain in the morning having got up early will be spent feeling sleepy and making no progress with work and study. But surprisingly that's not the case, and I feel like my mind is even sharper than during the day.

The morning light shines in through the window and steadily fills the room with a certain freshness, anticipating the start of a pleasant day.

Our lives often require us to decide on the spot what we're going to do. At times when we can't prioritize or adapt to sudden changes, we panic and everything gets out of control. The life of a monk, however, is very different; the flow of each day is decided from the beginning.

The pattern is established, which means that monks rarely feel at a loss about what to do next or panic about needing to do this or that. They simply focus on what lies in front of them at all times.

By getting up early each day and using the quiet time you have created for yourself to concentrate on study or work, you too can start spending each morning like a monk.

If you have already achieved something before heading out for your day at work or school, you'll be less flustered about the challenges that lie ahead.

Besides, having some time in the morning that goes uninterrupted by anyone else is a positive in itself. Your phone sometimes rings between nine and twelve at night, but it hardly ever rings between four and seven in the morning.

Rise early to spend quiet time in one of modern life's last remaining sanctuaries.

The early morning
is the quietest time
of the day. Rise early to
make use of this precious time by
getting ahead with work or study, or
simply enjoy being alone without
interruptions. This will take
pressure off the rest of
your day.

CLEANING

The Japanese have long valued the act of cleaning as more than just a chore. In Japanese primary and secondary schools it's normal for all of the students to clean, but elsewhere this is something students rarely do.

In Japan the act of cleaning is not simply designed to remove dirt from walls and floors but is also thought of as a way of teaching students how to polish the inner surface of the mind.

When you go to a temple in Japan you will find that the grounds are neatly kept. This is partly out of respect for visitors, but for training monks who live in the temple cleaning itself is ranked as one of the most important Buddhist practices.

In any temple that takes in ascetic monks you will not find objects scattered around, even if that temple receives few visitors.

If you observe temple activity even for a short while, you are bound to see monks wearing Buddhist work clothes known as *samue* each cleaning their assigned areas in silence. You can tell they are not thinking, 'Cleaning is such a hassle and I'd rather not be doing it, so let's just get it out of the way as quickly as possible.' They value it as highly as reading sutras and studying.

Let me tell you a story about Buddhist cleaning that you won't forget, even if its main character might.

There's a Japanese vegetable called myoga, or Japanese ginger. It's a strong-smelling plant, and legend has it that you'll become forgetful if you eat too much. This is because of its association with a particularly absent-minded monk called Chudapanthaka.

'SWEEP THE DUST, REMOVE THE DIRT'

During the Buddha's lifetime, there were two brothers among his disciples: Mahapanthaka and Chudapanthaka.

The elder brother, Mahapanthaka, was very clever and learned the Buddha's teachings well, but Chudapanthaka was slow to learn and unable to remember his own name, let alone learn the teachings of Buddhism.

Mahapanthaka worried for his younger brother and devised ways to somehow help him remember the teachings, but nothing he tried ever worked. Come the afternoon, Chudapanthaka would have completely forgotten what he had learned in the morning.

'A person who is aware they are a fool is a person of wisdom. A person who is unaware they are a fool is truly a fool,' said Buddha to Chudapanthaka, and he instructed him to sweep with a broom while chanting, 'Sweep the dust, remove the dirt.'

From then on, in rain and snow, in the sweltering heat and the freezing cold, Chudapanthaka continued to clean without a single day's rest, all the while chanting, 'Sweep the dust, remove the dirt.' Then one day, he realized, 'That's it, the dust and the dirt are attached to my heart.' And thus Chudapanthaka finally reached enlightenment.

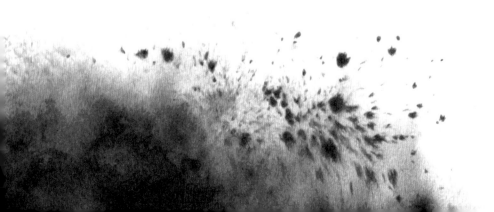

When he died it is said that a rare grass sprouted from Chudapanthaka's grave. This plant was named 'myoga', which literally means 'a person who carries his name on his back'.

This story teaches us that walking the path of Buddhism doesn't mean learning many things. It means being thorough in whatever you do. Chudapanthaka cleaned in earnest, and in doing so he was finally able to reach enlightenment.

A Zen master once told me, 'Cleaning is not merely labour, it is an important part of training.' At Zen temples, both new and elderly monks devote themselves to carrying out their duties together. When I heard this, I began putting more effort into cleaning.

The space in our offices and around our desks is our own training area where we set ourselves to work. At the very least, we want to try and keep these areas tidy, almost like cleaning a *dojo*. If you can prepare your mind and body in a setting completely free of dirt, then you may make new discoveries.

In Buddhism cleaning is an important spiritual practice. Doing seemingly menial tasks properly is a path to enlightenment. Working in a clean, tidy, well-ordered space is motivating and inspiring.

Walking
the path of
Buddhism
doesn't mean
learning many
things. It means
being thorough
in whatever
you do.

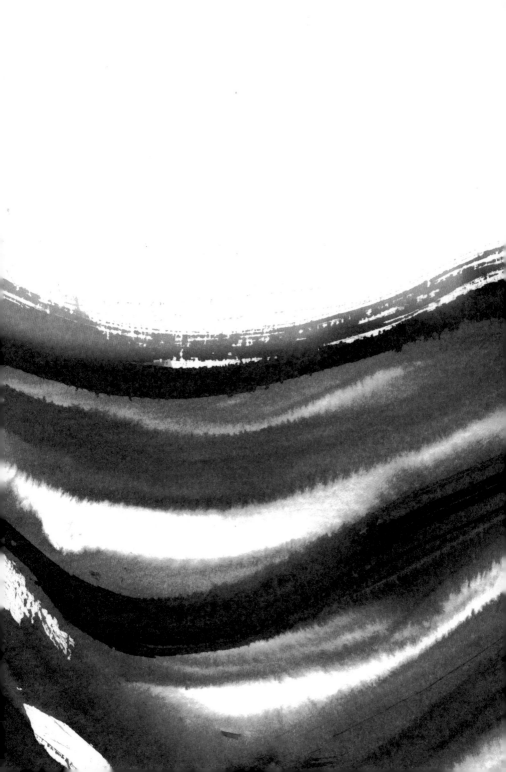

3
TRAINING
THE MIND

EATING AND
GRATITUDE

What sort of things do you pay attention to when doing your food shop?

I try to pay attention to the sell-by date, ingredients, where the product came from and how it was made.

Eating is the most basic human activity, and since what we eat ultimately becomes a part of our bodies we should treat it with more care than anything else.

Buddhism is strongly associated with vegetarianism, so many people believe that monks are prohibited from eating meat, but that's not actually true. It's even said that on occasion the Buddha himself ate meat.

When the Buddha reached enlightenment, it is said that he drank the milk rice given to him by a maiden called Sujata, and it appears that he would also accept meat when offered as alms. According to one theory, his death was caused by diarrhoea from spoiled meat that had been offered to him by a follower.

At that time, Buddhist precepts didn't stipulate that meat must not be eaten, although there is one rule forbidding the killing of living creatures.

We are permitted to eat meat if it is not from 'an animal that saw the place it was killed, an animal that heard it was to be killed for the sake of the monk himself, or an animal that is suspected of either of these'. Any food given as alms must be gratefully accepted.

So the question now is not what to eat, but rather what feelings you have when eating the food that you're blessed with every day.

GIVE THANKS FOR EACH MEAL

Instead of taking each meal for granted, accept it with gratitude. This type of Buddhist attitude can also be seen in the daily lives of Japanese people. The custom of giving thanks for a meal by clapping our hands together and saying, 'Itadakimasu' – literally 'I humbly receive' – is a wonderful part of Japanese culture that I would like to teach to other countries around the world.

No matter what you're eating, a lot of life has gone into every single item on your plate. So it is right that we express our gratitude towards the life that has gone into our food, and this is something I hope we will all continue to teach our children in the future.

When short on time, I'll grab a quick bite to eat at a fast food place and there have been occasions when I have suddenly realized that I forgot to give thanks beforehand.

In the end, no matter how much of a hurry we are in, I hope we can all find the time to fully appreciate the blessings of the food we eat, put our hands together and say, 'Itadakimasu.'

Food is a great blessing and should be received with gratitude. Never forget the life that has gone into the food you eat, whether animal or vegetable. Put your hands together and say, 'Itadakimasu.'

CHOOSING FROM A
MULTITUDE OF OPTIONS

About ten years ago, when I was still a high school student in Hokkaido, I imagined that living in Tokyo would be very exciting and I had no doubt that every day would be full of fun.

Sure enough, when I came to live in Tokyo as a university student I remember it all being very stimulating. I encountered a great variety of people and shops and it felt like the possibilities of life were endless. My university was near Shibuya, and it was so lively and noisy that every day was like a festival.

However, when we really think about it, no matter how many possibilities there are, we can only choose one thing at a time. And wherever we live there are only twenty-four hours in a day, and there's a limit to how much we can fit into that time.

No matter how many people we meet, there are only so many we can make friends with, and there are only so many places we can go.

HOW MANY OPTIONS DO YOU REALLY NEED?

There are so many more options than we can ever make use of, which means that we waste a lot of effort whittling down the candidates to make our final selection.

Bookstores are lined with guidebooks of all genres, and how-to books appear to be selling well. This could be a sign that our choices have grown too many, and people are now troubled by this.

Today's digital society overflows with information, and if we want to reduce our confusion then to some extent we must consciously control the information we receive. If we seriously scrutinized every available option we would spend our time doing nothing else.

LEAVE THE CARDS UNTURNED

Let's try comparing our choices to cards.

If you see cards laid out in front of you that haven't been turned over, it's hard to resist turning over as many as possible. However, if you spend all your time doing only that and neglecting what you're supposed to be doing, you're mistaking the insignificant for the essential.

In earlier times, there weren't as many cards to turn over and so we were better able to focus on what was in front of us. Then, when the occasional card fell from the sky it would have been something worth reacting to. But now that the world seems to be teeming with cards, we need courage and self-control to ignore them.

We must not become processing machines controlled by the information – we must control the information. I think it's important for us to determine our priorities and find ways to narrow down our options. Lately, I've been trying to come up with my own ways. For example, whenever I'm not using my computer I disconnect the internet.

In Buddhism, we are warned against neglecting what's important in life while getting caught up in the day-to-day rush. It's easy to forget that our lives are not going to last forever and end up wasting our days being chased by the small problems that are right in front of us, mistaking the insignificant for the essential.

The ability to choose from an array of options can feel empowering. However, if we spend our lives sifting through information to make our choices, it is the information that gains power over us. Learn to control the amount of information that you receive.

DEALING WITH THE INTERNET

In the previous section, I talked about the courage you need not to turn over the 'cards', or the options, that lie in front of you. But we can't live without turning over any at all, which means we need to choose which ones to turn.

This is easy to do if you simply reduce the effort required to turn the cards. If you cut down the number of cards from one hundred to ten, that means only one tenth of the effort is needed.

But in practice this doesn't really work, because you're more likely to locate the one card you find acceptable when turning over one hundred cards than when you turn over only ten.

So if you're going to cut down the number of cards, you'll have to increase the likelihood of finding a card you're satisfied with. The skill is to avoid any 'joker' cards that are irrelevant and better left unturned.

For example, when looking for information, we tend to start with an internet search. The times have changed considerably, and these days even primary school students use the internet to do their homework.

Reading, writing and arithmetic are no longer enough, and now we also need to learn information literacy. Although 'literacy' refers to the ability to read, 'information literacy' is the ability to make proper use of necessary information to meet your particular objectives. Part of this skill is to avoid unnecessary information that's better left alone.

In Buddhism, we are warned against neglecting what's important in life while getting caught up in the day-to-day rush.

STAY AWAY FROM ILL INTENTIONS

The internet is overflowing with information. Now we no longer have to rely solely on the information delivered to us by traditional media such as TV, newspapers and magazines, but we can also easily access information in blogs and other such sources that have been published by individuals.

These bring us material and viewpoints that aren't covered by the mass media, but on the other hand they also provide a lot of vague, misleading and false information.

Taking place in real time and without any geographical limitations, online gossip spreads everywhere like wildfire. The number of people suffering from online slander is increasing, and malicious rumours have become a social issue throughout the world.

A lot of this information, as well as being unnecessary, can also have a negative impact on the reader.

This problem isn't just limited to the internet; it's also the same when we seek advice from real people. While some will give us useful opinions, there are also those who give inoffensive but not very meaningful ones. Then, even more troubling, there are some who give opinions that are full of malice and cause upset. How should we deal with this kind of malicious information?

A basic coping strategy is to train your mind to a level where it will never become agitated, no matter how much troublesome information you access and no matter how many troublesome people you meet.

However, this is somewhat difficult to do. It's hard to stay calm when faced with malice, especially if that malice is directed towards us.

I would like to suggest a different, more manageable way. What we should do is come up with ways to consciously avoid that kind of information as much as possible.

Consider the following words, which can be found in the Sutta Nipata scripture:

'Not consorting with fools,
consorting with the wise,
paying homage to those worthy of homage:
This is the highest protection.'

We can easily get lost when we have relationships that tempt us towards negativity, and so it's important that we make an effort to distance ourselves as far as possible from those kinds of connections.

The internet can be a great tool, but it can also be an incredible time-waster. Worse, if we encounter online slander it can cause us distress. It's hard to read malicious opinions without becoming upset, so it's better to steer clear of them if we can.

A WANDERING MIND

I've always said that I am my own person and I take orders from no one. I have the intention to think and act the way I want, but when I really think about it that's not what happens in reality. I have a strong desire to do things my own way, but a desire is all it is since I don't actually know how to make this happen.

As an example, I'm constantly thinking about something or other. Even if I say to myself, 'It's been a long time since I've had some time off, so let's not think about anything today,' I still end up thinking about something every time. On the other hand, I just can't stay focused even if I remind myself to think something over. Despite not being disturbed by anybody else, I quite often find that I am unable to make myself do what I want to do.

For example, when studying a foreign language you might get distracted by something while looking up the meaning of a word. Before you know it you're reading a book that has absolutely nothing to do with the language you're studying.

Various thoughts wilfully float into our heads despite our knowing it's better not to think them. When we leave things in this state, we seem to fall under the illusion that we are thinking and acting how we want.

If I pay extremely close attention, when I leave my mind alone I notice all sorts of thoughts wandering into it.

There are rare occasions when this can be constructive, but mostly these random thoughts just jump about all over the place.

If we leave our minds unchecked, the noise in our heads will well up as and when it pleases.

According to a famous saying, 'It's hard to tell a poor thinker from a sleeping one,' meaning that if you don't have any worthwhile thoughts you'd be better off asleep.

The trouble is that it's hard to notice when your own scattered mind is performing 'badly'. Since we don't take notice, we steadily continue in this way, regretting and dwelling on things that are no use thinking about.

FACE WHAT YOU SHOULD BE DOING

Buddhism teaches us that it's in our nature to think about things we shouldn't be thinking about.

Once, there was a disciple who asked Buddha various questions such as, 'Is the world infinite?' and, 'Do people exist after death?' How do you think the Buddha replied? The correct answer is, he didn't. The answer to a question that cannot be known is meaningless, no matter how much you think about it. Losing your head over those questions is not just pointless but can be damaging. The Buddha's stance that there is no possible answer to a meaningless question is also apparent in one of his most famous stories, the Parable of the Poisoned Arrow.

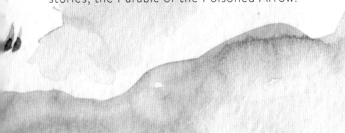

Suppose that a man has been shot by a poisoned arrow, and is on the verge of death. His friends have called for a doctor, but what if the man were to say,

> *'The arrow must not be removed until I know*
> *what kind of person shot me,*
> *what kind of bow shot me,*
> *and what kind of arrow has injured me.'*

While the man was concerning himself with these questions, the poison would travel and the man would likely die.

What Buddha wanted to convey in this parable is that time and time again human beings get themselves in a tangle discussing unanswerable questions when really there's no time for such things and we must face the reality that's in front of us.

We should not lose sight of the Buddha's original purpose, which was to end real-life suffering.

DON'T ASK 'WHAT IF?', ASK 'WHAT NOW?'

It seems like this attitude could be quite useful even when applied to the smaller questions and worries that we have on an everyday level:

'What if I fail the test and get rejected?'

'What if I get laid off from work?'

The reality is we must tackle the immediate problems, like how to prepare for the test or how to do our job as well as we can.

There are questions that we can't help thinking about, but it's pointless to consider them. So if we find ourselves thinking about them we must consciously stop.

If we leave our minds unchecked, the noise in our heads will well up as and when it pleases. Let's shut out this noise and instead focus on what we should be doing.

In doing this, you'll be sure to make far greater progress than usual in both work and study.

Our minds are easily distracted. We are often tempted to speculate on questions about the future that we cannot possibly answer or dwell on regrets from the past that we cannot do anything about. Stay focused on the here and now.

LEARNING FROM
YOUR MISTAKES

Everything has a cause and an effect. This logic is naturally obvious to anyone, especially if you're a modern-day person who likes to think rationally. Surprisingly, however, there are many people who are unable to properly grasp this concept.

Let me give you an example. When I was a student I was interested in the stock market, so I opened an online account and had a go at buying shares.

Within the space of just one day, the prices would move considerably as shares were bought and sold. The value of my relatively modest portfolio would move up and down from a few thousand yen to ten thousand yen or more.

I was kept on tenterhooks the whole time I had the shares, never knowing the right time to sell. In the end, I kept hold of them for too long and I lost tens of thousands of yen. What did I tell myself at the time?

You're probably thinking it would be something like, 'This is the result of my own inexperience and greed, so it can't be helped. I'm paying for my own mistakes.'

But this was by no means what I thought. I blamed my failure on other people, like the politicians whose bad decisions caused the economy to get worse and financial journalists whose bad advice I followed.

There's a cause for every effect, but we rarely turn to look at the actual cause: our own immaturity.

FACE THE TRUE CAUSE

As you can see from this example, while modern-day people claim to value logic, they often have thoughts that defy logic.

Failures that are clearly our own fault are an inconvenience to us, and so we try to push the responsibility onto something else.

It's troubling when something happens and we don't know why, and so we have a weakness for taking something that's completely unrelated and twisting it into a plausible cause.

But if we keep blaming the wrong thing we'll keep making the same mistakes. Each time we will wonder why and our anxiety will grow and grow. Therefore, it's important to keep the law of cause and effect in mind at all times.

When things go wrong, it can be hard to acknowledge that we have made a mistake and we blame other people. Learn from your own mistakes or you will keep repeating them.

ACKNOWLEDGING YOUR DESIRES

There are a variety of temptations all around us, such as food, alcohol, tobacco, shopping and more. From time to time, we resolve to confront those temptations. We diet, stop drinking, quit smoking, start budgeting and so on.

Whenever new methods are developed to fight temptation, what is and isn't effective becomes a popular topic of conversation. We especially hear lots of outrageous dieting strategies and they nearly always fail.

Even if they appear to work in the short term, there's often the issue of rebound. While this can be a problem with all diet methods, it's especially so for those that claim the most extreme results, like 'Lose 10 kg in one week!' Yes, you may lose 10 kg in one week, but if you then gain 20 kg two weeks later it will all have been for nothing. From what I can tell it's not that bigger results have a bigger rebound, but more that if you forcibly suppress your desires there is sure to be a rebound later on.

Let's consider our own experiences. For example, what happens when you want something but you forcibly suppress those feelings?

Imagine that although you really want the latest technology, you convince yourself that you don't and that it's of no concern to you.

You won't gain any awareness or understanding of your desires if you try to act like this. Forcing yourself to pretend your desires don't exist will eventually become too much to bear, and the front you put up will collapse.

It is true that Buddhism urges us to extinguish our destructive emotions. However, that is the ultimate aim; leading up to that point, learning how to 'get along' with those emotions will become more useful than how to 'extinguish' them – particularly for those of us who are not practitioners of Buddhism and lead average lives.

GAIN AWARENESS OF BEING SWAYED

Extinguishing your destructive emotions is different from ignoring them. Pretending you don't care about some delicious-smelling food is completely different from declining the source of the smell.

Therefore, unless we are great practitioners of Buddhism we must approach this issue based on the assumption that it's not possible for us to extinguish our destructive emotions.

Knowing that we are controlled by these incessant destructive emotions, we should look for ways to work around them – for example, by preparing each of our surroundings in order to avoid being swayed by desire wherever possible.

If you want to go on a diet, then one way to do this would be to avoid going to places where you'll be surrounded by the smell of your favourite sweet treats.

When your destructive emotions inevitably well up, don't turn away from them. Instead, start by being fully aware of the fact that there are emotions within you that are simply impossible to override.

Of course, for illnesses such as alcohol dependency where we can't get better without proper medical care, then we must seek treatment. But even then, the first step on the road to recovery is to gain an awareness of the situation.

If you're unaware of being swayed by these emotions you can't manage them. Why not seek a more realistic method that uses awareness? This will avoid the relapse caused by pretending your desires aren't there. If this living creature we call the 'self' cannot be controlled as a whole, then, as a whole, we won't be able to achieve good results.

SAY A PRAYER OF RENUNCIATION

There's a traditional Japanese custom in which someone who wants to give up something they like prays to the Buddhist or Shinto deities for their heartfelt wish to be realized.

I think it at least helps reduce the chances of a relapse.

For example, imagine your doctor orders you to stop drinking and smoking. This would be particularly difficult for someone who previously regarded alcohol and cigarettes as essential. However, what if you were to make a promise to the Buddha?

Even if you could face the all-seeing Buddha and make up bold excuses, you would only feel miserable. The Buddha is probably the best companion as you follow through with your resolutions while being conscious of the depths of your own destructive emotions.

Destructive emotions are the inner enemy that threaten our tranquillity. It's impossible to vanquish this enemy completely, and if we ignore it, it will double in size and run riot. Far better to learn how to make the enemy your ally.

Suppressing your desires never works. Instead, acknowledge them and try to work around them by keeping yourself away from temptation as far as possible. Another method is to say a prayer of renunciation to the Buddha. That way you will have to answer to him if you relapse.

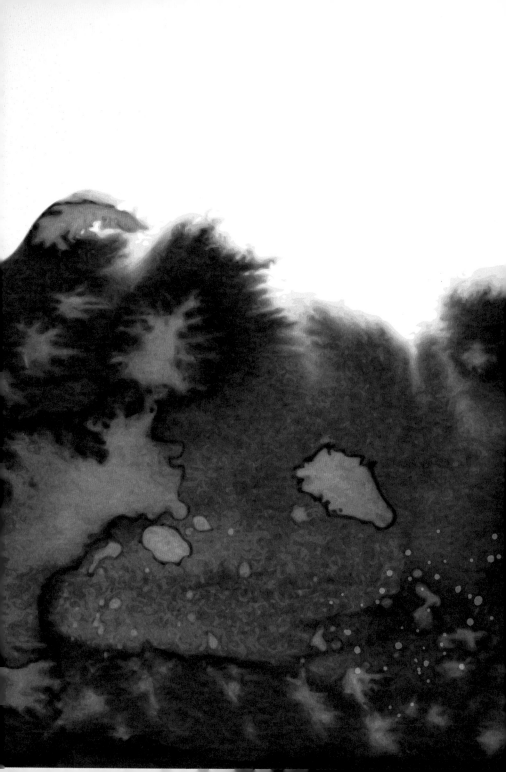

4
LETTING
GO

MONEY

Of all the various stimuli around us, there's one that is particularly troublesome: money.

Since it's connected to every aspect of our lives, nobody is able to stay away from it.

Money itself is nothing but pieces of paper. Unless we exchange it for goods and services it's completely useless – it can't even be used as a notebook. Often, we can't even touch it; it's just a number on a screen or a bank statement. And yet, people are more or less fixated on this number.

If it increases, we are happy. If it decreases, we are sad. As children, we are taught how society works and told to save up for the things we want to buy. But as adults, we may develop a tendency to save money just for the sake of having money, rather than to buy something we want.

People work their very hardest to increase this number, and they try to make efficient use of the money they save to increase it more and more. On the other hand, there are those who use too much and fall into debt, and they must then find a way to pay back the person who lent them that money.

In this case, people work in the service of money because they have to return what they borrowed from somebody else's pocket.

It seems appropriate to say that money has taken up a position of control over our actions.

DON'T MEASURE YOUR WORTH
IN TERMS OF MONEY

Why is it that money has such a hold over our minds that we can't let go of it?

For one thing, the basic nature of money is that it offers the possibility of being exchanged for all sorts of goods and services. We feel somewhat comforted to have money, as this allows us to preserve that possibility for the future. It's like storing plenty of rice down in the cellar.

There's also another aspect to money. As well as its practical function as a token for buying goods and services, money has come to be used as a common criterion for measuring the value of all sorts of things – including humans.

Increasingly, we use how much money we have or earn as a means of comparing ourselves to other people. So money is no longer just the rice in our cellar, it has become a signifier of status.

Comparing ourselves to others is a huge obstacle to living peacefully. In Buddhism, this comparison is said to trigger the destructive emotions of the three poisons (see page 20) and will always lead to a sense of superiority or inferiority towards others. We may find ourselves thinking things like, 'Thank goodness I'm wealthier than this person,' or, 'How can that person's salary be double mine?'

Our minds become agitated and we enter into a race against other people. This competitive urge to climb higher begins a cycle of self-perpetuating desire where we keep wanting more and more.

Comparing ourselves to
others is a huge obstacle
to living peacefully.

MAKE MONEY WORK FOR YOU, NOT THE OTHER WAY ROUND

When we want money for the sake of having money, we become slaves to money.

If you want to live your life freely and peacefully without being bound by anything, then you need to avoid going to the extremes as best you can and remain stable, using as much self-control as possible.

In order to do this, it's important to maintain and improve your sense of balance so that you can save and spend the right amount of money for you– not too little, not too much. But what I really want is for everyone to stop wondering whether what they have is a little or a lot of money, and to stop using this as a means of comparison against others.

We all need some money, but if you become overly preoccupied by it you'll never have a peaceful day.

> Money is nothing more
> than a token to be
> exchanged for goods and services.
> However, if we desire money for
> its own sake and use it as a means to
> compare ourselves to other people, then
> we become its slave. Freedom from
> desire for money
> is priceless.

THE COMPARISON IMPULSE

Comparing ourselves to others is a more deeply ingrained habit than we would imagine, and it rears its head each time we unexpectedly think about something.

We always express our worries about ourselves by comparison to other people: 'That person's younger than me, but they're already so successful,' or, 'They got married ages ago, but I'm still single.' These things are only an issue because of how we compare to other people.

Is a person's happiness something that can be compared to others'? A lot of people would probably say no. But the fact is, there are various kinds of rankings in this world that we make a fuss over, anything from test scores to annual income.

Since each person has their own personality and the environment in which they're placed is different, it's no use comparing one person's happiness with another's. Although everyone surely knows this to be true, still it's difficult to stop measuring ourselves against other people.

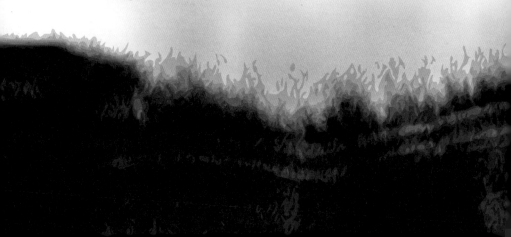

It's hard to feel
envious of yourself.

It's only natural that this will all go wrong since we are trying to force a comparison between things that fundamentally cannot be compared.

If you think of yourself as better than other people you'll come to be content in living with feelings of superiority. If you think of yourself as less than other people you'll come to feel miserable and jealous towards others. Either way, only ugly, negative emotions are born, and nothing good can come from that.

IF YOU WANT TO COMPARE, COMPARE WITH YOURSELF

So what should you do when, against your better judgment, you feel like comparing yourself to others?

For a start, you should push aside those feelings and tell yourself that you are you and other people are other people. If looking at rankings stirs up feelings of superiority or jealousy, then don't look at them.

However, the comparison instinct is embedded in all of us and it won't be silenced as easily as that.

So why not come up with a person – the only person, in fact – against whom you can make valid comparisons? That person, of course, is yourself.

Try thinking about how your present self compares to your past self, and how your present self should compare to your future self.

For example, if you're concerned about your annual income try comparing your present income to your past income, rather than to somebody else's. It may have gone up, or it may have gone down after losing your job.

But even if your income has temporarily lowered, it's hard to feel envious of yourself. If you're dissatisfied with your current situation set reasonable goals for your future and work towards them.

THRIVE ON FEELINGS OF COMPARISON

Now, just because you are you and others are others, this doesn't mean you should have nothing to do with other people. Rather, you should actively involve yourself with those who are able to maintain their own pace and do their best. Together you can become comrades who support each other.

Even in the world of Buddhism, where each of us walks as an individual, we actually value those who walk the path alongside us. Moving forward isn't possible without other people who can help guide us in the right direction and offer encouragement.

In the same way, it's extremely important for us to have friends with whom we can work to reach our goals and who will show us the way when we feel disheartened.

Some people may also have 'rivals', usually in their work environment. What does this type of rival mean to you? Personally, if it's in the good sense where you encourage each other while staying true to yourselves, then it's not a bad idea to have one.

If you're both doing your best to improve your business performance, then when the other person achieves a new sales record you'll think to yourself, 'If they can get those results, perhaps I can, too.' This then acts as inspiration, helping you to set achievable targets for yourself.

We influence one another as comrades who are each competing against ourselves. In contrast, competition against hostile opponents who only compare results to those of other people and look to outsmart and defeat others will stop us from making progress in the long term.

Comparing yourself to other people only leads to feelings of superiority or inferiority, neither of which are good for you. Instead, compare yourself to your past or future self. Seek comrades for mutual support on your path. Rivals can be a positive influence if you use their achievements as inspiration for your own.

COLOURED
GLASSES

It is often said that we see the world through coloured glasses. Rather than seeing things honestly and fairly, we evaluate them from a prejudiced point of view through lenses that are tinted by a mixture of our own self-interest and emotions.

However, unlike actual glasses, we cannot take these figurative ones off. Each person's vision of the world is unique. People may look at the same picture but the impression it makes will vary from person to person.

And, unlike actual glasses, we often do not realize that we are wearing them, or, if we do, we assume it's easy to remove them whenever we want.

Let's take the newspapers as an example. People reading the same news article about a legal case will react completely differently. Some will sympathize with the plaintiff, others with the defendant. Each will believe that their own views are fair and correct. Naturally, it's also impossible for the article to have been written from a neutral perspective, since it was written by a human.

Even if the report is written with a scrupulous effort to be impartial, the prejudices of the journalist and newspaper company will still come through. The colour of these prejudices may be pale but it will still be there. Nevertheless, we treat news reports as objective fact.

Human objectivity will always be more or less tinted.

THINK FOR YOURSELF

If we're unsure of our own views we shouldn't rely on other people's.

People who don't listen to others and are defiant in their own judgments and prejudices are troubled, but those who say they can't make judgments for themselves are even more so.

Although it's good to get advice from someone who has rich experience, you must not forget that in the end the one who will make the decision is you. We cannot blame other people for our own mistakes.

Acting on forms of divination like fortune-telling can also be quite dangerous. Even if you later blame the gods or the Buddha when things go wrong, the failure is nevertheless your responsibility. My life can only be lived by me. I cannot hand over the reins to someone else.

Before the Buddha died, he said to one of his disciples, 'Do not rely on me, but rely on the Dharma.' In other words, treat the Buddha as just another person whose advice you should not accept unquestioningly. Instead, lead your life by thinking for yourself and following the Dharma, the universal teachings of Buddhism.

GET TO KNOW YOUR PREJUDICES

These coloured glasses are unreliable, and although we dislike them we cannot take them off. We also can't rely on anyone else. So what should we do?

If we cannot take our glasses off, no matter how much we try, we have to find a way to live with them successfully.

Since we cannot see things from a fair and proper perspective we cannot grasp the truth of what we are looking at. If that's so, why don't we start by getting to know the features of our own coloured glasses?

Compare the colour of other people's glasses with our own. When looking at a picture, you may see one thing while someone else sees something else. Don't think about which perspective is right, just consider how the perspectives differ.

By doing this, little by little you'll come to understand the characteristics of your own coloured glasses. You will then learn how to walk an honest path even under the influence of your various preconceptions.

What's more, by gaining a greater understanding of other people's perspectives we can broaden our capacity for compassion, and we will have fewer needless disputes.

We all view the world
through coloured glasses
tinted by our own experiences
and prejudices. We cannot change
this, but we can learn to take account
of our preconceptions. No matter how
unreliable our view, we should base our
decisions on our own judgments
not anyone else's.

AUTHENTIC RELATIONSHIPS

Whether in the workplace or at school, few things give us more concern than our relationships with other people.

Relations between bosses and staff, between co-workers, between teachers and students, between seniors and juniors, and between classmates. There must be many people who feel awkward and stressed.

So how can we make our relationships less stressful? Maintaining a certain distance from someone we don't get on with could help. But this isn't always possible. If we're working in a close-knit team it would be strange to keep one of the other members at arm's length.

It's not about the distance between yourself and others but more a question of being honest with yourself about your feelings towards them.

OUT OF SIGHT, BUT STILL IN MIND

Trying to maintain a physical distance from people we don't like is one thing. However, it's a very different story when it comes to mental distance.

If I were to ask you to list three people you dislike, certain names would probably come to mind straight away. No matter how far away from these people you have managed to get, the fact that they have sprung to mind means they must still have a considerable presence within your consciousness, and so actually they're close by.

If you can't resolve those feelings of dislike, then, no matter how much time passes, they will remain a source of noise within your mind. You must ask yourself why you feel that way, determine the cause from within your own mind, and then overcome it.

We may say we don't know the reason for not liking a person, but there must be one somewhere. Funnily enough, the people we dislike are often those who are most similar to ourselves in some respects. As it is often said, one person's fault is another's lesson.

If you can determine the cause of your dislike and uncover the process that led you to this way of thinking, then you'll be able to create a new, more honest and authentic relationship with this person.

LOVE FOR THE RIGHT REASONS

Now let's try thinking about those people we do like. Love towards other people is normally viewed as a positive emotion but in Buddhism it can be a form of attachment, which is thought of as a destructive emotion associated with greed.

You're probably wondering why love is viewed in such a negative way, but Buddhism isn't necessarily saying that love itself is bad – it's the direction that matters.

The kind of love that comes from a compassionate and merciful heart is to be encouraged. However, love that is directed at yourself, in other words narcissism, is a destructive emotion.

On first glance, whether it's a romantic relationship or not, having affection for someone else appears to be love directed at another person. But there are many cases where it can, in fact, be love directed at yourself.

For example, when you say something like, 'I like them because they're good-looking and kind,' this reveals more about what we gain from being with that person than about how much we care for them, and involves feelings of loss and gain.

Then, if the reality turns out to be different from what you had imagined, you say that you have been betrayed and love suddenly turns to hate.

If we can ensure that our love for other people comes not from narcissism but from a compassionate and merciful heart, we will be surrounded by relationships that are good for everyone involved.

Buddhist teachings say that it's important to have good companions, but that we should not assess these people according to whether we like or dislike them. Rather than friends who are convenient for you, it's important to have friends with whom you can grow together, all the while giving each other encouragement. Such relationships are the key to a refreshing life.

Being honest with yourself about why you dislike someone will help you build a more authentic relationship with them. Make sure that your love for other people is founded on a genuine concern for them, not on what they offer you.

AN UNEXPECTED LIFE

Buddhism teaches us that 'life is suffering.' Here, 'suffering' is more than putting up with adversity or pain — it represents things not turning out the way we want.

In Buddhism, we observe the four universal sufferings of life, which are birth, ageing, sickness and death. While we all know that these sufferings are inevitable, they often occur at times and in ways that we do not expect.

We are constantly suffering from things not turning out the way we want. Even when things occasionally do go the way we want them to, we soon frame new expectations and so the relief from our troubles is only temporary.

We bring a large part of our distress on ourselves by trying to get our own way, despite life being something that doesn't go to plan.

One solution is to realize our own limitations and understand that life doesn't usually turn out the way we expect. We might think that we can still try to have things go the way we want, but it's this thought itself that represents our own limitations.

Ironically, I believe those who are more self-disciplined are more inclined to worry about things not turning out as expected.

An irresponsible person will be quick to give up. Their attitude will be, 'Well, it didn't work out. I was just unlucky this time. Let's try something else.'

On the other hand, a serious person who works painstakingly hard will ask themselves, 'Why is nothing going well for me when

In order for us to be freed
from the distress of human
relationships, we need to face
the reality that not everything
will go how we expect.

I'm following the plan and working so hard?' Those who are able to exert a certain level of control over themselves will try to exert control over the rest of the world.

Strike a balance between these two extremes by telling yourself, 'If it goes the way I want, it's a blessing.' This attitude allows us to pursue our goals with determination, but without becoming too upset if they elude us.

RECOGNIZE THE LIMITS OF YOUR CONTROL

It may be obvious, but regardless of whether it's husband or wife, lover or friend, other people are other people. We cannot assume that they will behave in the same way as us, and we cannot treat others as our own property – not even our children.

Human beings place a great deal of value on being able to have their own way. We try to expand the territory over which we feel a sense of control as far as possible.

Things going your own way results in pleasure, and things not going your own way results in displeasure. We try to grab hold of as much of this pleasure as possible, whether in terms of money, land, possessions and so on, and pull it in towards ourselves.

Therefore, in order for us to be freed from the distress of human relationships, we need to face the reality that not everything will go how we expect. This approach is to understand the limitation of our existence by nature. However, this doesn't mean we shouldn't care how things go. If things don't turn out the way you want, take those results on board and learn from them for next time.

Accept the results wholeheartedly, even if they are different from your expectations. Whatever happens, tell yourself, 'Life is good. Everything is in perfection.'

This approach extends our existence to the cosmic level. You're saying, 'If that's what happens, that's what I wanted.'

In any case, the door to a solution should open if you look closely at the relationship between yourself and life's events.

No matter how hard we try, we cannot guarantee that things will turn out the way we want them to – and they generally don't. Don't let your happiness depend on events you cannot control. Instead, accept whatever happens, learn from it and keep going in hope not expectation.

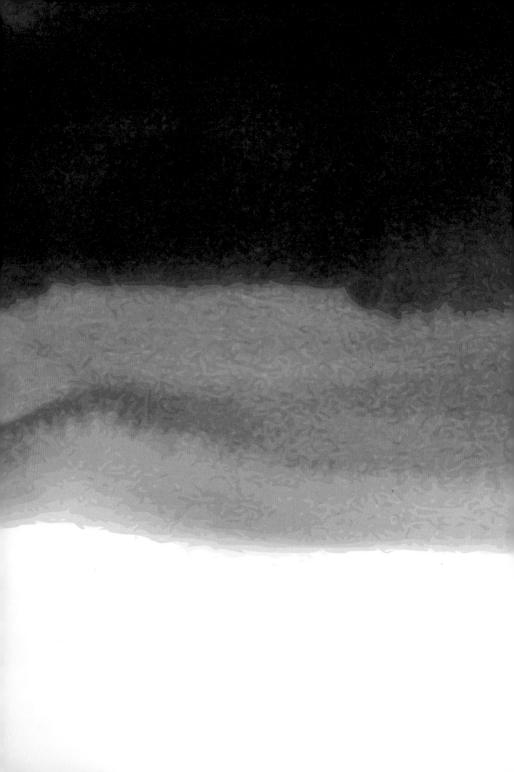

5
'DO NO EVIL, DO GOOD'

'DO NO EVIL,
DO GOOD'

If you were to sum up Buddhism in one go, what would you say?

There's one phrase I would use to answer this question:

'kusalassa upasampadā; sacittapariyodapanam,

etam buddhāna sāsanam.'

This translates as, 'Do not what is evil, do what is good, and purify one's own mind – these are the teachings of Buddhism.'

Known as the Verse of Admonishment of the Seven Buddhas, this passage is from one of the early Buddhist sutras, Dhammapada, and its message is convincing and simple for all who see it. You might think that summarizing the essence of Buddhism shouldn't be so easy, but let me tell you a famous story about this passage.

Long ago in China, there was a man called Bai Juyi. He was famous as a poet, but also showed exceptional skill as a politician.

There came a time when Bai moved to Hangzhou to take on a new post as prefectural governor. He decided to pay a visit to Zen master Daolin, a highly reputed monk from the area. In order to test Daolin's abilities, Bai questioned him about Buddhism.

'What is the essence of Buddhism?'

Daolin's response to this was, 'Do not what is evil, do what is good, and purify one's own mind – these are the teachings of Buddhism.'

'Even a three-year-old child knows that,' replied Bai, exasperated that Daolin appeared not to be taking his question seriously.

'This may be something that even a three-year-old child knows, but it is also something that even an eighty-year-old man cannot put into practice,' retorted Daolin.

ACCEPT THAT YOU'RE NOT PERFECT

Indeed, it's just as Daolin said. Although this is something that everybody knows, putting it into practice is another thing altogether.

There are many who want to try and avoid doing bad things, aiming to do good and live with a pure mind. It is not simply that

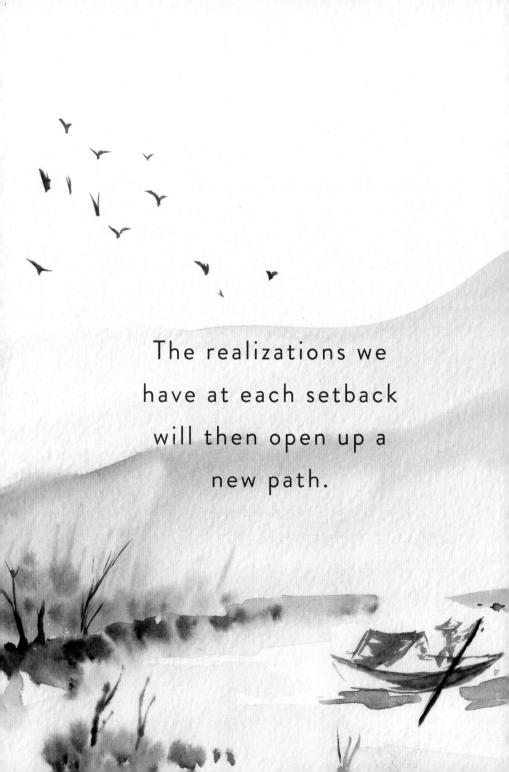

The realizations we
have at each setback
will then open up a
new path.

we recognize these as moral principles but also that, deep down in our hearts, we are searching for that way of life.

Almost nobody would actually think to themselves, 'I want to become someone who's disliked by others and live life maliciously, never missing a chance to do harm.'

There are perhaps some people who grow terribly bitter throughout their lives, but I doubt even they would wish for their own child to grow up to be a bad person.

I believe this is because we all know instinctively that we shouldn't do bad things and that if we do something bad we won't find happiness. Do not what is evil, do what is good. This seems easy, but is actually difficult.

However, it's not something we can give up on. Even if it's hard to get it right every time, you should still do what you can. What sort of things do you become aware of when you try doing this? It feels as though this is the question with which the Verse of Admonishment of the Seven Buddhas confronts us.

EXPECT SETBACKS

Can you go even a short while without doing anything bad? Even if we tell ourselves that we aren't going to, we may step on an insect or say something hurtful to another person.

On the other hand, although you may think you're doing something good by giving up your seat to an elderly woman on the train, or by handing in a wallet you found on the street to the police, it may not amount to much if we ask how much it's worth.

Making an effort to do good and avoid doing bad can cause us to grow conceited and then sometimes we suddenly realize that we hold contempt towards others who are unable do the same.

Each time we adopt this noble attitude to avoid doing bad things and try doing good, we experience small setbacks. The realizations we have at each setback will then open up a new path.

Whether you're emotionally calm or you feel as though you're losing sight of yourself, I hope that without fail you can remember and appreciate these words.

'Do not what is evil, do what is good, and purify one's own mind – these are the teachings of Buddhism.' Easy to remember, hard to do. But still worth trying.

We all know instinctively that we shouldn't do bad things and that if we do something bad we won't find happiness.

GAINS AND LOSSES

How do we usually think and act? For many, I believe the most important motivating factor is the calculation of gains and losses.

And it's not just shopping where we make decisions based on what we stand to gain or lose. Another time would be when a child worries over whether it would be more fun to tag along on their sister's outings, or play games at home with their brothers.

Our interest in gains and losses shows up in every choice we make while going about our daily lives, and we can probably all come up with one example or another.

If someone tells you that they don't make decisions based on what they stand to lose or gain, then I would take what they say with a pinch of salt. It would be great if it were true but, sadly, such a person is hardly found in this world.

Of course, that's not to say that human behaviour is decided by this calculation alone. We also act out of personal curiosity, as well as noble motives such as beliefs and a sense of justice or responsibility. If we look through history, there have been people who have risked their lives for either their religion or country, not for personal gain.

Nowadays, it has become more common for us to consider, and act in, our own interests first. What's more, even things which we were once unable to put a price on can now be bought and sold using money. Putting a monetary value on everything makes us even more inclined to calculate our gains and losses.

In Buddhism, it is believed that the more you receive the more you'll want. I think this is something that we all instinctively know.

'DO NO EVIL, DO GOOD'

If you gain ¥1,000 you'll want ¥10,000. If you gain ¥10,000 you'll want ¥100,000... Human greed is essentially this cycle on repeat and if you leave it unchecked it will never stop. Happiness fades when we are controlled by what we stand to gain or lose.

However, all too often in today's bustling world we base our decisions on short-term financial considerations, despite not knowing what the implications will be in the long term. Companies prioritize profits over sustainability, and employees jump from job to job in search of the highest salary.

It's now too late to suggest that we should stop calculating gains and losses, as this has become the rule by which modern society works.

BE GENEROUS

Although we can't change the world we live in, why not occasionally try resisting this interest in gains and losses to avoid being controlled by it? By breaking free from this principle which manipulates our behaviour on a daily basis we will be able to see ourselves objectively, and this should lead to a stillness of the mind.

For example, as a way to counter your own interest in gains and losses, why not do the opposite of what you usually do? Instead of using your money, time or possessions for yourself, offer them to other people. Through 'letting go', we should be able to learn about the state of our own attachments.

Many religions disapprove of making decisions based on gains and losses and incorporate the act of letting go of possessions for

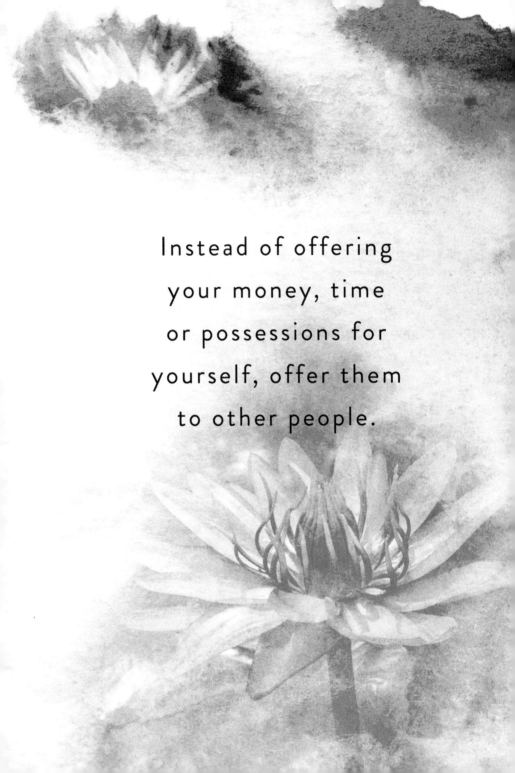

Instead of offering
your money, time
or possessions for
yourself, offer them
to other people.

the good of the world into their practices. In Buddhism, there is a concept of generosity known as fuse. In Islam, there is a custom of alms-giving known as zakat, and charity is also valued in Christianity.

Even among successful celebrities who have built themselves a fortune, the number of people who actively practise letting go is increasing. Many musicians and Hollywood celebrities are passionate about charity, and in the business world you'll no doubt be familiar with people like Bill Gates and Warren Buffett, who have set up charitable foundations and donated most of their assets.

Likewise, some people work hard to make money in the first half of their lives, and then do their best to give it generously in the second.

This doesn't mean that the more you give the better. If I let go in a way that suits me, then that's plenty enough. Daring to let go of the things you treasure and care too much about will often lead to awareness.

Modern society conditions us to base our actions on what we stand to gain or lose. Try to resist this tendency. Be generous. Let go of the things you treasure.

LIES, DUPLICITY, ABUSE
AND IDLE SPEECH

In Buddhism, there are ten evil deeds that we as humans should avoid doing. Although they are called 'evil deeds', they aren't evil in the sense that they are punishable by law. In Buddhism, 'evil deeds' refers to actions that will result in future suffering.

On the other hand, not doing such actions is considered a good deed that will cause no trouble and instead bring joy.

However, I would like to note here that in Buddhism 'joy' and 'suffering' carry somewhat different meanings from the ones we are used to.

When we say, 'Good deeds bring joy,' the word 'joy' does not denote a fun, carefree feeling, such as the sheer bliss we experience when entering a hot spring, or the fun we have when going to Disneyland. Likewise, when we say, 'Evil deeds bring suffering,' we are not using 'suffering' to describe the bitter, painful feeling we get when we do difficult or stressful work, or when we recall bitter memories from our past.

Put simply, 'joy' in Buddhism refers to a peaceful and clear mind surrounded by the lightest light; while 'suffering' is a troubled and confused mind surrounded by the darkest dark.

It's worth noting that four of the ten evil deeds are deeds of the mouth – that is to say, they are committed through words. As it is often said, 'Out of the mouth comes evil.' Now let's look at the four – Lies, Duplicity, Abuse and Idle Speech individually.

LIES

When we tell a lie our hearts and minds become troubled from the very moment we let the untruth slip from our mouths. Lie detectors record these uncontrollable changes in our heart rate and brain activity and reveal our suffering (in the Buddhist sense) for all to see.

It is sometimes said that, under the right circumstances, a lie may be justified. However, we should aim to lie as little as possible, and if one does slip from your mouth apologize as quickly as you can and try to make amends.

DUPLICITY

This is when we say something that we later contradict. It is sometimes referred to as speaking with a forked tongue.

Duplicity is similar to lying, but the problem with it is not so much that we are saying something that is untrue, rather that we are saying different things to different people.

We must always follow through with our promises and be consistent in what we say. If we are duplicitous we will lose the trust of those close to us and wind up isolating ourselves. We might even call it duplicity when superiors in the workplace constantly change what they say depending on the day, causing those who follow their instructions to get flustered, not knowing what to do.

ABUSE

This refers to speaking ill of others.

It doesn't matter if we're telling the truth or how consistent we're being, we mustn't use words that belittle others, such as calling someone dumb. It's a truly horrible feeling when you hear that someone has been saying nasty things about you behind your back.

This not only troubles the mind of the person who has been insulted, but also the person who said it and those who listened. There may be some people who say that insulting someone will make them feel better, but please consider this for a moment.

It's true that when speaking ill of someone, you may feel a slight rush.

However, looking down on another person and speaking ill of them to lift yourself up is a rather distasteful practice, and there's no doubt that this is an 'evil deed' which creates noise in the minds of everyone involved.

IDLE SPEECH

This refers to the use of embellished language.

Flattery is a typical example of this. Rather than considering what is best for the other person, we try to take advantage of them by tactfully using flowery language that feels good to hear but doesn't reflect what we actually think or twists the truth.

You may think that flattery is actually a good deed, since it makes others feel good and allows them to enjoy themselves. But we must not do it if we are saying it because of what we stand to gain, and not for the benefit of the other person.

In the famous Hans Christian Andersen story *The Emperor's New Clothes*, the foolish emperor is taken in by his tailor's cunning flattery and winds up embarrassing himself, which is what can happen when we engage in idle speech.

WATCH WHAT YOU SAY

We are all guilty at times of these four evil deeds of the mouth, myself included, but we can prevent a considerable number of misdeeds by being aware of them and by paying careful attention to our words on a regular basis. Please give it a try – there's no doubt that it will do some good.

The four evil deeds
of the mouth are lying,
duplicity, abuse and idle words.
In each case they disturb the
minds of the person committing the
misdeed and the people on the
receiving end. Think before
you speak.

INSULTS

Insults unsettle the minds of those they are aimed at and those who say them. They allow us no peace, but still they have a certain attraction that makes us want to say them despite knowing they are wrong. For example, everyone has probably had at least one experience where they get together with friends and somebody speaks ill of someone who isn't there, and then everyone else piles in.

Friendship groups may be founded on mutual interests and characteristics, but they may also be based on mutual enemies. When friends get together to speak ill of their enemies, this strengthens the solidarity of the group.

Sometimes, when the group has exhausted all the bad things they can think of to say about their mutual enemy, an individual who had been a member of the group up to that point is set up as an enemy and made the next target of abuse.

BREAK THE CHAIN OF MALICE

Insults fired from one person to another arouse our sense of curiosity and cause a negative chain reaction.

They are a problem for the person who says them, but also for those nearby who go along with them. When that wave reaches you, do what you can to stop it travelling any further.

Although social media can be a great force for good, they are also, sadly, an excellent vehicle for groups who wish to speak ill of their enemies. Groundless slander posted online can reach hundreds, thousands or even millions of people in an instant. The more people it reaches, the stronger it becomes and the more opportunities it has to grow even bigger. If the person speaking ill is anonymous, the intensity grows.

When reading online posts, we see people furiously hurling insults at others despite not knowing the full story. They are blind to their own faults and we wonder who on earth these people are, but when we suddenly come back to reality we realize that we are also blind to our own faults. In any event, the ill will catches on.

There may be times when we become the target of the attack. When I hear that someone is speaking ill of me, it makes me angry and hurts my feelings.

Through twisted curiosity, I then want to know exactly what words were used against me. Once I find out, I bear ill will towards that person, setting off a negative cycle.

LET IT GO IN ONE EAR AND OUT THE OTHER

When someone bears ill will towards me and either directly or indirectly speaks badly about me, I must not take it too seriously.

If we do take such things seriously and try to protest or retaliate, all that happens is that we enter a vicious circle. Pay as little attention as possible to it, and try to carry on as though nothing has happened. It's not necessary to hear the details of what was said. However, it's best not to completely ignore the insult, either.

Wilfully ignoring it is another form of protest, which could backfire and intensify the ill will. The best plan is to head in a direction that will discourage people from continuing to speak negatively about you, putting a stop to the growth of the ill will.

This technique of letting ill will go in one ear and out the other can stop it in its tracks. Better still is to follow the fundamental Buddhist attitudes of not lying, not constantly saying things to please others, not speaking ill of others and not giving false flattery. Those who have mastered these teachings are less likely to become the target of abuse in the first place.

If you are in a group that is speaking ill of others, you may be afraid that by breaking free from the group you will become the next target. Find the courage to leave the group. If you do it the right way, without rancour or confrontation, no one will be able to say many bad things about you.

> If you find yourself in a
> friendship group that insults
> other people, put a stop to the ill
> will or quietly leave the group. If you
> become the target of ill will, let it go in
> one ear and out the other. By avoiding
> the four evil deeds of the mouth, you
> will be less likely to be treated
> this way.

COMPLAINING

If there's something we aren't pleased with or find unpleasant, then we complain. Although complaining won't improve the situation, we continue regardless. The person who is listening might be able to offer advice but they won't be able to solve the problem – and they might not stick around for very long, because associating with people who moan is depressing.

We first met the destructive emotions known as the 'three poisons' in chapter one. One of these, *moha*, written as 愚痴 (*guchi*) in Japanese, was originally a Buddhist term used to refer to the stupidity of being unable to understand or judge things

People who
complain may think
of it as a 'necessary
evil', but in fact it's
just an evil.

correctly. Nowadays, this word is also used as part of the phrase 愚痴を言う (*guchi wo iiu*), which means 'to complain'.

It makes sense that complaining has come to be associated with *moha*, as wasting time and energy bemoaning our misfortune demonstrates our inability to understand the situation we are in.

In any case, Buddhism teaches us to avoid *moha*. However, such stupidity does not readily disappear from the world.

Despite knowing that complaining is a negative action which we would be best to avoid as much as possible, there are many who think that an occasional moan, perhaps over a drink, is a useful way to let off steam. In reality, however, it has the opposite effect.

The three poisons are extremely powerful and stubborn, just like weeds that keep growing back no matter how many times we pull them out. Even though it may be difficult to do away with greed, anger and stupidity, it's important that we try to suppress them.

However, complaining is like giving water and fertilizer to these weeds. Far from weakening them, it makes them grow even faster. Then the seeds from these weeds blow over the fence into the gardens of those who have to listen to your complaints.

VIEW COMPLAINING AS A LOSS

People who complain may think of it as a 'necessary evil', but in fact it's just an evil.

One characteristic of evil is that it can escalate. Take violence as an example. A minor scuffle can soon get out of hand. It would be wise to nip it in the bud while it's still small.

If you find it hard to picture complaining as an evil, consider it instead as a loss.

I only consider things in terms of gain and loss rather than good and bad. I'm always thinking, 'I don't want to lose, I want to win.' So by labelling something I shouldn't do as a loss, I'm able to suppress my impulses better than ever before. I realize that this inability to judge things correctly makes me the embodiment of stupidity, but it works for me! Above all, complaining is a waste of time.

If you have a spare moment to grumble, you could use that time to do something more worthwhile. Interpreting things in a negative way won't solve your problems.

People who have a tendency to complain will become disliked by those around them. At work, if all you do is complain you'll lose the trust of your co-workers and miss out on important opportunities.

When someone needs an important task to be done, they won't choose you if they think you're going to complain about it behind their backs. They'll opt for someone with similar qualifications who will happily accept the work with a smile.

So by complaining you stand to lose time, friends, credibility and opportunities.

Having negative thoughts and feeling sorry for yourself is the start of a vicious circle. At such times, let's try changing those feelings and expand the circle of smiles.

Complaining does us no good at all. We may think it helps us let off steam, but it actually makes us feel worse. It wastes our time, alienates our friends and drains energy in the workplace. Look for things to be grateful for, not to complain about.

6
WALKING
YOUR OWN
PATH

LIVING BY YOUR
OWN RULES

I like Buddhism for its freedom. I think it's good that it doesn't force its ideas onto people.

It's not a case of simply believing in the 'right path' shown to us by great people. Rather, Buddhism is a style of teaching where we walk alone, going through the process of trial and error. Only later do we realize which was the right path.

If I were to pull on the hands of those who have no interest and force them to walk, they would not be walking the path at all. So, although it may seem like a carefree approach, we can do nothing but wait until someone makes up their own mind and says, 'I want to walk the path.'

It's important to make decisions for yourself in all walks of life, not just in Buddhism. We know from our own experience that things generally turn out much better when we do something we have decided to do, rather than being forced to do it.

For example, a child who is told to study for a test will do so reluctantly and half-heartedly, whereas one who decides to study for themselves will focus. This results in entirely different outcomes. Even if these two children somehow end up with the same test scores, they will have completely different paths to walk from that point onwards. Although the former may have managed to pass the test, having studied as they were told to do, if they do nothing but follow instructions from other people, then once they enter society they may become the sort of person who is unable to act on their own initiative.

On the other hand, the one who got into the habit of making their own decisions from childhood will likely be able to handle all kinds of situations when they become an adult. They will be able to go at their own pace without being misled by others and overcome the challenges they face.

The important thing is that you do not unthinkingly follow other people's opinions and rules, you also accept them personally and act accordingly.

THE PRECEPTS THAT GIVE US SELF-CONTROL

Although Buddhism doesn't force its rules on people, it does still have rules. These are known as 'precepts'. Among them are the following five principles:

- No killing – you must not kill any living creature.
- No stealing – you must not steal other people's belongings.
- No false speech – you must not lie.
- No sexual misconduct – you must not have indecent relationships.
- No intoxication – you must not drink alcohol.

All Buddhists should keep these precepts in mind and follow them, but Buddhism itself does not prescribe any punishment for not abiding by them. The important thing is that if you're a Buddhist you should aim to make your own decisions and stick by them.

Of course, it's not a bad thing to just go ahead and follow them simply because they're rules. But actually, if we were to say whose benefit these precepts are for, then they're for no one but ourselves. This is something we come to understand as we repeatedly obey and violate them day after day.

For example, I believe all of us from time to time have done something wrong and been unable to apologize honestly. Instead, we have tried to downplay our actions and gloss over the truth of what we have done. What sort of feelings do you have at times like this?

I believe we regret what we have done, and come to suffer as the noise grows in our minds. Even if you're able to withstand the noise, your mind remains dark for a long time after. Later, when you think you have forgotten about it, something may trigger your memory and bring back those unpleasant feelings.

Of course, the person we have wronged will also have unpleasant feelings about the experience. Once the mind is troubled, it's not easily settled.

UNDERSTAND THE INTENTION BEHIND THE RULE

The point is that we have to accept responsibility for whether or not we obey these precepts.

No matter what kind of rules they are, don't simply obey them because they are the rules, and don't simply ignore them because you don't feel like following them. Think about the intention behind the rules and, if you agree with that intention, make an effort to obey them for your own sake. That way, you'll be able to obey those rules while seeing them in a positive light.

On the other hand, if you do not agree with the intention behind a particular rule you might choose to disobey it (although you will need to be prepared to accept any punishment that comes from breaking the rule).

It's not a case of simply doing whatever you are told to do. We should carefully consider what it actually means to follow rules, and by absorbing this into our inner selves we will be able to deal with life in a more calm and steady manner.

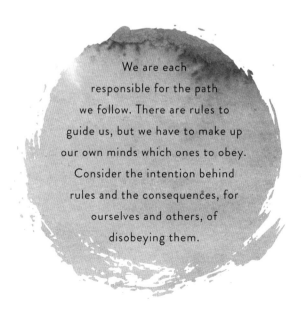

We are each
responsible for the path
we follow. There are rules to
guide us, but we have to make up
our own minds which ones to obey.
Consider the intention behind
rules and the consequences, for
ourselves and others, of
disobeying them.

TAKING A
STEP BACK

We live in a world overflowing with material comforts, but not everyone finds life comfortable. Thanks to medical advances, our physical health is protected like never before, but many people are mentally stressed.

The number of people suffering from mental illnesses like depression, and the number of people who take their own lives, continues to increase year by year.

I have no doubt that we have reached a point when many people must radically reconsider their way of life. We must seriously question whether our current concepts of wealth and happiness are right.

Simply realizing that the path we have been running has led to a dead end is, in itself, a big step forward. It gives us the opportunity to change course, while others continue running the wrong way without realizing it.

This was something that I myself managed. My mind used to be almost completely occupied by so-called worldly values; that is to say, I tied my happiness to material and economic wealth.

Although I pretended to know that such things weren't important, deep down this view was not easily changed. However, since my life has been touched by Buddhism, my way of thinking has come to change little by little.

Material things are no longer that important to me, and instead I have begun to place more and more value on the cultivation and enrichment of my mind.

Cultivating the mind means
taking a good, hard look
at yourself.

FACE THE HUNGRY GHOST

Cultivating the mind means taking a good, hard look at yourself. In this respect, Buddhism works like a mirror; it draws our attention to all aspects of ourselves, both attractive and unattractive.

Thanks to this process, there have been some small changes in my mentality. As the worldly riches that once weighed on my mind have become fewer, it also feels as though the stress caused by my surroundings has lifted somewhat.

This doesn't mean I have become indifferent to the world – rather, I have become able to take a step back and think about things from other people's perspectives.

My basic nature hasn't changed much. As the Buddhist myth states – a hungry ghost who has looked in the mirror and seen their ravenous greed will behave a little differently from one who has never done so, even if they are otherwise the same.

With greed comes stress, but if we can take a step back we will be able to reduce that stress to the point where it hardly affects us.

'THE CAUSE OF EVERYTHING LIES WITHIN MYSELF'

There are three strategies for dealing with stress:

- Distance yourself from the cause.
- Boost your resistance towards the stress.
- Destroy the cause.

For example, imagine there's someone at work who causes you to feel stress and whom you can't help but dislike.

There are ways you could distance yourself from that person to reduce the stress, or you could perhaps practise relaxation techniques to help you cope with the stress better. You could conquer the stress in your own mind by getting to the bottom of why you dislike the person and why they cause you stress.

The Buddhist approach focuses primarily on the last method. Look within your own mind to find the ultimate cause of your confusion and then overcome it – that is to say, extinguish your destructive emotions.

I know that this is awfully difficult for those of us living normal lives within society, but even if it doesn't work completely it still might be worth trying. Worldly stresses can be lightened with the help of a little Buddhist inspiration.

Take a step back from your own viewpoint and put yourself in the position of the other person for just a moment. We still won't be able to say that we like them, but the feelings of dislike won't be as strong.

BE COMPASSIONATE

Cultivating the mind has a positive effect not only on yourself but also the people around us.

Buddhism teaches us wisdom and mercy. Wisdom is not merely knowledge, it is the ability to perceive all things exactly as they are, and a wise person will naturally have a compassionate heart.

In Japanese, the word for 'compassion' is 慈悲 (jihi), made up of 慈 (ji) meaning 'to bring joy to others', and 悲 (hi), which means 'to remove suffering from others'. Another Japanese expression meaning 'compassion' is 抜苦与楽 (bakku-yoraku), or 'removing pain, giving joy'. This is the Buddhist practice of taking away the anxieties and fears from those who are afraid, leaving them without fear. In so doing, you also relieve your own stresses.

When you come to a dead end, this is your chance to stop and cultivate your mind. Why not look to Buddhism for ways to relieve your stress?

Conquer your stresses
by taking a step back
and recognizing what is causing
them. Cultivating your mind can help
you understand the stress caused by
pursuing material wealth and can help you
appreciate the viewpoint of people you
dislike who cause you stress.
It will help you to become more
compassionate.

THE MIDDLE WAY

The society we live in thrives on creating desires. Strangely, it would no longer function if everyone were satisfied.

Buddhism teaches us that human desires can never be satisfied; if we stimulate them, they just keep on growing. The more we get, the more we want.

At first, our desires are like a tiny flame, but if we add fuel to the fire that flame will grow, spread and never die out.

A society based on desire is, in short, a society in which no one can be truly happy so long as they remain faithful to the system.

This is a society that encourages us to stimulate our desires to the maximum while competing fiercely with others, telling us that this is necessary for our growth. Isn't there something wrong with that?

Buddhism recommends what is called the 'middle way'. We should neither head in the direction of pointless suffering, nor should we run towards hedonism. Rather, we should take the path that lies in the middle, without going to extremes.

The Buddha himself became a priest at the age of twenty-nine. After six years of severe asceticism, he abandoned austerity and reached enlightenment. What he was unable to realize while following an extreme path was revealed to him when he switched to a moderate course.

When I first learned about the middle way, it didn't click with me straight away. I was hoping for something rather more precise than just 'Avoid the extremes and go down the middle.'

However, as I grew to know a little more about Buddhism, I gradually came to realize the true depth of the middle way.

MOVE FORWARD WHILE WATCHING YOUR STEP

In our society, there are some people who pursue the extreme path by letting go of their desire to win the competition and rise above the rest. But as I mentioned earlier, it's clear that happiness doesn't await those who keep pushing forward but don't know where they are going.

The extreme path is also the easy path. On the other hand, I have come to realize that although taking the middle path sounds easy, it is in fact very difficult.

It's easy to trace your finger around the edge of a circle, but it's surprisingly difficult to point exactly at its centre. Moreover, we are living in a society that changes from moment to moment, and as such it has become a sort of polyhedron. This makes it even more difficult to walk down its middle than to follow the outer edges.

As we walk along the path straight towards our goals, we are required to be both careful and perceptive.

The capitalist ideal of pursuing your desires in competition against others is being shown to lead to a dead end, so I believe that the middle way will become even more influential in future society.

There's no doubt that we humans cannot afford to go to extremes, since we don't even know our own selves all that well.

When we adorn our lives with countless possessions, we are being controlled by our ever-growing desires and this deepens nothing within us. Our short lives could come to an end with our having only touched the outer edges of ourselves.

In an age when many think extremes are more exciting, I believe true innovation is born from the middle way.

In a sense, those on the extreme path are on a runaway train going round in circles, while those on the middle way are walking straight towards their goals. Which do you prefer?

The middle way is a path between the extremes of self-deprivation and self-indulgence. It is not easy to follow the middle way, as we are forever being tipped towards one extreme or the other. Keep a firm footing and a clear view of where you are headed.

Buddhism teaches us that life isn't what we expect it to be. It also encourages us to live positively and thrive.

POSITIVE THINKING

Many people claim to use positive thinking to overcome the absurdities of life and achieve the outcomes they desire. Of course, I also prefer thinking about things in a positive way. After all, nothing good comes from thinking negatively.

But please don't misunderstand – thinking positively doesn't mean that everything will go the way you want.

There are times in life when it's futile to tell yourself, 'Give it your best! You can do it if you try!' Sometimes, we are opposed by forces in society that are far more powerful than our individual efforts.

Then, if you make yourself work too hard, it's quite possible that you could exceed your limits without realizing and suddenly feel crushed.

I was once invited onto a radio show and asked, 'What do you do when you hit a wall?' And so I explained, 'There are times when no matter how hard we try, we cannot get to the other side of the wall. When you simply cannot get over it and you're about to be crushed by it, there is also the option of running away.'

Buddhism teaches us that life isn't what we expect it to be. It also encourages us to live positively and thrive.

The Buddhist way of thinking is to consider things in a flexible and positive manner, regardless of the situation and whether things are going the way we want them to or not.

KEEP CALM AND CARRY ON

Of course, living life in a serious and logical manner is never a bad thing. Plodding along down your own path is a common method for living a peaceful life without confusion.

However, no matter how hard we try to keep up our own pace in life, we will always face some unexpected, unavoidable setbacks – perhaps we lose our job because the company we work for goes bankrupt or is restructured. At times like this, it's only natural that we should think, 'But I've been working so hard, why is this happening to me?'

Sadly, hard work will not enable us to get over an insurmountable wall. The more serious a person is, the more distressed they might become when met by such absurdities. When struck by these kinds of emotions, let's try to stay calm.

We build everything up step by step, plodding along through life with great effort, and to then see it all collapse is very painful. With many years of effort disappearing down the drain, it's understandable that we feel despair.

But at times like this, let's take ourselves to the next step using the Buddhist way to positive thinking.

Whatever you have been putting your efforts into until now will never be in vain, no matter what happens. Someone who has been able to do their best and keep their own pace without drifting towards the easy path will be able to continue doing their best, even if the focus of their efforts changes.

It won't be difficult for such a person to find another job, and they'll also get help from those around them.

Remember, though, that attitudes such as 'I'm still better than them,' or 'There are still a lot of people beneath me,' have no place in positive thinking from a Buddhist perspective.

Comparing yourself to other people will not lead to a happy future. When you make a mistake, it's understandable that you feel frustrated and say things like, 'If I stumble now, I'll get left behind.' But if you compare yourself with others you will never be free from frustration for the rest of your life. Your own troubles are what's important, not those of other people.

'If you change, the world will change.' This is the Buddhist way to positive thinking.

Thinking positively won't make everything turn out the way you want. Trying hard is not always enough. The Buddhist version of positive thinking involves staying calm in adversity, picking yourself back up and going again. You can change direction while keeping to the middle way.

THINKING FOR YOURSELF

Once seen as uniformly middle class, Japanese society has become more unequal. But one thing that hasn't changed is the sense of security Japanese people get from doing the same as everybody else.

Mocked for their conformist mentality, the Japanese typically follow suit whatever the situation, reject anything that's different and fear rocking the boat.

Of course, to say that we should each act completely differently from everyone else is an individualistic fantasy. However, taking the stance that it is always best to just do as others do can lead to a dead end. If you follow your neighbour and end up tripping over them, it's your fault not theirs.

The issue isn't whether we live our lives the same as or differently from others, and it doesn't matter if we sometimes do things the same as the person next to us. The issue is whether or not we are thinking for ourselves.

It's important that we continue to calmly ask ourselves how best to deal with the situation, and how we should live our own lives from this point onwards.

When we ask ourselves, 'Am I doing this right?' we become anxious and start worrying about what other people are doing. In the end, we stop thinking for ourselves and get pulled into the current that flows around us. We then lay the blame for this on others as well.

However, even if you ultimately decide to make the same choices as your neighbour, you must think carefully and reach this conclusion yourself.

ENRICH BOTH HEART AND SOUL THROUGH WHOLE-BODY EXPERIENCES

So, why must we think for ourselves? If we don't think about what we are doing, going with the flow without really knowing why, then the way in which we digest that experience will be completely

different from if we had made the decision ourselves, even if we end up having exactly the same experience.

By going through experiences with your whole body and properly digesting them, the next time you're faced with the same situation you'll have a better experience and understanding than before.

For example, if we read a book and then read it again many years later, we may find that we understand parts that we didn't before, or that this time a different section resonates with our hearts.

This is evidence that during the time in between, we have come to digest various experiences. However, if all we have done during this time is float along and follow suit, then our understanding will not have progressed. It's important that we internalize our experiences, enriching our heart and soul.

It is said that Ananda, one of the Buddha's disciples, was closer to the Buddha than any other attendant. But despite hearing more of his stories than anyone else, he was unable to reach enlightenment during the Buddha's lifetime.

One possible reason for this is that he was too close to the Buddha and became deeply dependent on him. While he listened to much of what the Buddha had to say, he may have been unable to internalize what he heard and learn from it.

Of course, that doesn't mean we shouldn't listen to what other people say. No, we should listen to all kinds of different opinions. However, don't swallow the advice you receive unconditionally; instead, bear it in mind and use it as a basis for your own thoughts. We mustn't rely on others.

I hope we can all make a habit of drawing together information to help us come up with an answer that we ourselves accept.

DON'T WORRY IF YOU REACH
THE WRONG CONCLUSION

Be careful not to be overconfident in the answers you come up with. The important thing is that you think for yourself, not that you come up with the correct solution.

It's also not always possible to judge afterwards whether it was a good or a bad decision. However, if you use your own mind to think hard and come up with an answer, then no matter what result you arrive at you'll be able to accept it and think about what you should do next time, correcting the direction you're heading towards. You'll also be able to realize the limitations of your thoughts.

If you didn't come up with the answer yourself you won't be able to accept the results and take the next step. Continuing to train your thoughts and judgments is useful for settling the mind, and gaining an awareness of your limitations is sure to teach you confidence and humility at the same time.

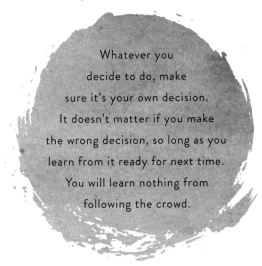

Whatever you decide to do, make sure it's your own decision. It doesn't matter if you make the wrong decision, so long as you learn from it ready for next time. You will learn nothing from following the crowd.

FOCUSING ON THE SELF

We make all sorts of choices as we go about our lives and choosing our career path is one of the biggest decisions of all.

I believe there are very few people who have absolutely no regrets about their career choice. Even a monk who has entered a temple and is determined to take over as the chief priest may sometimes worry that they will rebel and flee from the temple.

We are living in an era that celebrates individuality, and so it is natural that some people may want to choose a career that is distinct from everyone else's rather than one that will allow them to delve more deeply into themselves.

This is a mistake many of us make: we pay too much attention to the path and neglect to look at the self. We're too busy wondering which way to go and we completely forget about ourselves.

For me the true purpose of following a path is not to complete the path itself, but rather to learn about ourselves as we walk along it.

This idea is supported by the fact that the character for 'path' (道) features in the terms for such important aspects of Japanese culture as the tea ceremony (茶道), flower arranging (華道), kendo (剣道) and even Buddhism itself (仏道). These paths have been forged over centuries through the hard work and enthusiasm of many people. By following them, we discover not only a rich inheritance of skills and knowledge but also a view of the universe that encapsulates life.

Each path is completely different, but no matter which one you go down it will eventually lead to self-reflection.

I consider Buddhism to be a path within a path, as it encourages us to really look at ourselves and offers all sorts of guidance while we are travelling our life's path.

CONSIDER THE PURPOSE OF THE PATH YOU'RE WALKING

In choosing a path there are always various factors to consider. For example, when choosing a job, you have to consider the stability of the company, how high the salary is, the working environment and the growth rate of the industry. You must then bear the responsibility for the results of your choice.

But when walking your chosen path, if you lose sight of questions such as what the purpose is or who you are, then you're not actually walking it. This point doesn't only relate to our specific career choices.

Viewing life itself as a path, if you look only towards the conditions of what lies ahead and forget why you're walking the path or what sort of person you are, then it could be that you're not making the most of your life.

'Is it better over there?' 'Am I losing out over here?' While we constantly ask ourselves these kinds of questions, life quickly passes us by and then we die. Rather than walking our own path, we just end up being selfish.

'Selfishness' is generally used to refer to wanting to have your own way and acting self-indulgently, but its true meaning is something quite different.

Many people don't look at themselves properly, they just assume that they know themselves better than anyone else does. So the true meaning of selfishness is wilfully manipulating the body of someone we refer to as the 'self', even when we don't know the 'self' all that well. The first thing that we should look at is our own selves rather than the course we take, since we cannot have everything go the way we want – not even within ourselves.

When following the path of your career or your life as a whole, stay focused on yourself. It's easy to lose sight of who we are as we pursue our goals, but our achievements will ring hollow if we don't understand ourselves.

LIVING HARMONIOUSLY

Throughout the ages, religion has been one of the major causes of conflict in the world. In contrast, Buddhism is gaining attention for being a religion that fundamentally avoids conflict and aims for peace.

Rather than looking to oppose, Buddhism heads towards harmony. It doesn't go about making strong claims that it has the correct way of thinking; instead I like the way it demystifies its essence as 'nothing more than following the laws of nature, the natural order of things'.

Harmony is also a very important consideration for living our lives with a quiet mind.

We may be wondering about the direction of our lives in general, or we may be thinking about those everyday dilemmas where we just don't know what to do. One way to make a decision is to consider which option would result in the greatest harmony.

Left to themselves, human beings tend to think only of their own gains and losses. However, taking harmony into consideration is sure to produce positive results, provoking a sense of compassion towards not only ourselves and our surroundings but also the whole world.

Take driving a car as an example. I can't say why, but this often brings out people's personalities.

If I let myself be while driving, then the worst side of my personality comes to the surface and my driving becomes rough and careless. However, that sort of driving can be troublesome, or even dangerous, for those around me.

When I realize this is what I'm doing, I try to be conscious of harmony. I aim to drive as though I'm taking in the view not only from the driver's seat but also from an imaginary helicopter flying overhead. In doing so, I'm able to ride the flow of traffic smoothly, considerately and safely.

AVOID CREATING CONFLICT

The opposite of harmony is conflict, and in this world the number one cause of conflict is dishonesty.

Listening to the lies of other people is tiresome, but many will know from experience just how much telling our own lies can trouble our minds and disturb our harmony.

Suppose that as a child you're running around the house playing, only to break an expensive vase that your parents value. What if you hide the truth and instead blame the family dog you were playing with? Since dogs cannot talk, there wouldn't be any of the interpersonal conflict that would occur if you had blamed your brother or sister. But what if, because of that lie, the innocent dog is told off and punished by receiving no food?

Thanks to that lie, you escape punishment but you are overcome with guilt towards the dog. Although it may seem like the world is in harmony, your own harmony is disrupted.

No matter how skilfully you lie and get the better of the situation, it's only natural that you'll continually worry about your lie being exposed. That kind of worry is a huge weight on our minds. Even if we think we have forgotten about the lie, our fears may occasionally resurface in our nightmares. As long as you harbour a cause for anxiety, you won't be able to achieve true harmony.

Regarding how Buddhism views peace, the words of one of my teachers left a deep impression on me: 'What do you think is true peace? Is it now, when there's no war going on in front of you? Or is it when there's no war anywhere in the world? Or is it more than that even? The only way in which true peace can be achieved is when not only is there no war currently taking place anywhere in the world but all potential causes of future wars have been eradicated.'

This is also true for harmony. Not only is it important that we have harmony in the present but we must also make a constant effort not to create causes of future conflict.

Why not try focusing on harmony in your day-to-day life? It will surely help you live peacefully.

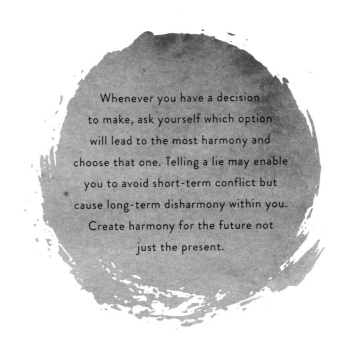

Whenever you have a decision to make, ask yourself which option will lead to the most harmony and choose that one. Telling a lie may enable you to avoid short-term conflict but cause long-term disharmony within you. Create harmony for the future not just the present.

'DEPENDENT ARISING'

Sometimes I feel as if our lives are getting shorter year by year. Of course, average lifespan statistics tell us that the opposite is true. However, something still doesn't seem right. I think what feels like it's getting shorter is the time available for meaningful experiences during our lives.

Whether it's in work or study, the competition is growing more and more fierce. If you can't keep running with all your heart and without looking back, you won't be able to reach the top.

Not everyone can be a winner, and it's a somewhat lonely and intense battle. Many people constantly feel that their place in

society is under threat. Despite living among a great number of other people, they are stricken by a sense of isolation and a feeling that they do not belong.

Yet still they keep running in the belief that this is the only way to live.

Truly this is a path that leads only to confusion. This takes several forms.

First, there is the confusion of not knowing where you want to go.

No matter how much you look at a map, if you can't decide where you're heading you can't make progress. If you set out walking anyway, this will lead you nowhere. You first need to calm down and decide your destination.

Another form of confusion comes from not knowing where you currently are.

If you keep moving despite not knowing where you are, you'll just become all the more lost. First you must come to a stop and then you can look at a map to try to work out your location.

Then there's the most basic form of confusion, which comes from not realizing that you were lost to begin with.

Everyone else is running, so you run with them in the same direction. You run with all your heart because you're worried that if you stop you'll get left behind. You don't know your destination or your current location. However, you don't have time to look back to see where you've been, so you just keep running.

The competition continues to accelerate, and so, too, does the confusion. The busier we are, the deeper the confusion.

It's important that we cultivate our minds alongside our pursuit of worldly success. This cultivation of the mind also means recognizing our confusion.

If we only pursue success, our minds steadily become more self-centred and our sense of isolation deepens. If we only ever look at the world through competitive eyes, we come to regard those around us as our enemies. This is a sign of being deeply lost.

In Buddhism, there is the concept of 'dependent arising', which allows us to overturn this competitive outlook on the world.

The busier we are,
the deeper the confusion.

The idea is that all things are dependent on each other; there is not one single thing that can stand by itself.

IF NO ONE ELSE EXISTED,
WE WOULD BE NOBODY

If we think about it, we are living in a network of connections. The relationships between husbands and wives, parents and children, brothers and sisters, teachers and pupils, friends and colleagues – our lives are supported by countless connections.

In order to become parents, parents need children; in order to become children, children need parents. That's right – if no one else existed, I would be nobody. This is also important when considering how to live peacefully.

Stillness of the mind isn't something we are able to achieve on our own. So long as we live in a society, we need to be able to still our minds alongside the people we are somehow or other involved with.

We automatically tend to think of ourselves as separate from everyone else, but in reality that's not the case. To one degree or another, we exist in connection to every single thing. I would cease to exist without these connections.

Think of the connections as sounds. If we are to achieve stillness of the mind, we cannot demand a world that is completely silent.

There is always going to be some kind of sound within the world. If we approach life in a competitive spirit the sounds we hear will be dissonant. It will then take considerable effort to try to drown out these sounds with one that is even louder.

However, if we take on the concept of dependent arising the unique sounds of our individual connections will combine in a wonderful harmony.

In the words of Shinran:

'When pure winds blow in the jewel-trees,

It produces the five tones of the scale.

As those sounds are harmonious and spontaneous,

Pay homage to Amida, the one imbued with purity.'

Although some of the tones in a scale are known to be dissonant, from the perspective of dependent arising they come to be heard as natural and beautiful.

Break down the egocentrism that is at the heart of our confusion, and feel the connections between all life in dependent arising. It is through these connections that you will find true stillness of the mind.

It feels like life is moving faster and faster and becoming more and more competitive. To still your mind amid such confusion, slow down and feel the connections you have with all other things. Listen for the sounds they make together in wonderful harmony and chime with them.

INDEX

PICTURE CREDITS

Shutterstock, Inc: pages 4–5 frankie's; 6 jekyma; 8–9, 71 ArtMari. 10–11, 19, 23, 25, 36–7, 53, 69, 72–3, 80, 94–5, 98, 100–1, 110, 116–7, 118, 140–1, 158–159, 162–3 Elina Li; 14 Noppanun K; 27 Gringoann; 28–9 FlaviaMarie; 32–3 Supergrey; 40, 59, 77, 142, 152, 171 Ola Tarakanova; 42–3, 48, 62, 84–5, 102–3, 120, 122–3, 135, 168–9 Sergey Pekar; 56–7, 147 Xinling yi fang; 86–7 Guy' s Art; 91 Anastasia Lembrik; 113 Elena Karnitskaya, 126 Noppanun K; 135–6 Supergrey; 154 Mushakesa

Senior Commissioning Editor
  Victoria Marshallsay
Translation Lauren Barrett
Copy editor James Hodgson

Designer Georgie Hewitt
Index Angie Hipkin
Production Gary Hayes